T0196659

"Male to Female"
"Wo–Man"

Veemala Victoria Persaud

authorHOUSE®

AuthorHouse™
1663 Liberty Drive
Bloomington, IN 47403
www.authorhouse.com
Phone: 1 (800) 839-8640

Published by AuthorHouse 07/27/2018

ISBN: 978-1-5462-5328-0 (sc)
ISBN: 978-1-5462-5327-3 (hc)
ISBN: 978-1-5462-5326-6 (e)

Library of Congress Control Number: 2018908927

Dedication

Reflecting with sadness on a once imprisoned soul,

a long list of tortured memories arises.

I PRAY, DEAR LORD ALMIGHTY, FORGIVE THE ONES WHO HAVE SINNED AGAINST ME, BUT MOST OF ALL, I BEG YOUR FORGIVENESS FOR ANY AND ALL MY TRANSGRESSIONS ONTO OTHERS. I PRAY FOR THE INNOCENT AND ASK THAT YOU PROTECT THEM FROM REPEATING ANY UNBECOMING BEHAVIORS THAT ARE. I HUMBLY BESEECH YOU. AMEN.

All of my love to Mom and my beloved siblings. I love you!

CONTENTS

Acknowledgements

To all whom have crossed my path I would like to give honor, respect and thanks to all that you have done for me. Your support and effort have helped me to build strength as I have exceeded the possibilities of love. To my mother, grandmother and family; I owe my due diligence for sticking by my side through the ins and outs of my journey. The love you give reaches to the depths of my heart. To all the friends I have encountered, thank you as well. Please know that so much of my uprising would not have been without you.

Thanks and Love.

Preface

I wanted the title of this book to greatly impact and inspire those who may need courage in their own lives. This book, *Wo-Man*, was written for those in similar predicaments who may need a boost of encouragement, support and hope. Perhaps those individuals who read the many stories to follow will come to know that they are more capable and more powerful than they believe. My motivation in setting all this down on paper, in speaking out, has been to help liberate all those who have endured trauma and pain as they survived the best they could from childhood to adulthood. This book is a collection of my life's extreme moments (extreme fear, sorrow, extreme joy) and of the people who touched my life. My life from its very beginning up until the present has been a wild rollercoaster ride. While writing this book I have journeyed through a landscape of memories and events that I had not always accepted or conquered. I hope it serves as a validation and source of comfort to all those facing and conquering their demons.

Introduction

From chaos to success, this is a story of the violence and abuse I have endured. A battle of identity, sex, pain and pleasure. I am still alive, alive to share my story and to encourage others. Hopefully my story will help others avoid the pain and torture that I have miraculously survived.

The feelings and emotions within each story may cause the reader to wince, grimace, and even weep in empathy. My feelings are a smorgasbord, ranging from desperation to delight. My self-imposed mission to reveal the truth requires the depiction of each and every one of these shades of emotion.

Every day I remain tortured: you will see. I, Veemala, have inflicted deep, dark hurt on others—but never intentionally. My heart is heavy, pulled down not by the violations of body and spirit I have suffered but also by the knowledge of the undeniable pain I have inflicted on innocent and blameless others.

As you read my story, try not to judge. Wait until the conclusion of my memoir. Then and only then can you decide…

Fact: bananas are one of the healthiest fruits, chock full of vitamins and minerals. They are often enjoyed in shakes, as part of a meal, or as a dessert—the way nature intended.

Nature never intended bananas to be shoved sadistically down a throat.

Imagine: four whole bananas suffocating you, choking you. Although you cannot breathe, you must not cry, must not break. *Impossible to imagine*, you might think.

All the while they laughed.

All I could think about…wrap my mind around…was *Breathe Veemala, breathe! Hold on…Fight!…even if only in your mind.*

That was my mantra: *Win, you must win.*

My mind urging my body to block the physical pain. I promise my almost lifeless body that there is hope, that there may be a better life ahead.

I emerged from these atrocities with questions.

Who am I?

Which one of the selves that I have created is the real me?

Should I conform to society's 'norms'?

Or can I truly be me?

Is there anyone out there for me?

Someone who will really care?

Someone who will understand me?

Someone who will accept me? Really and truly accept me?

My young, undeveloped mind could not grasp what was happening.

Why me? Why is it always me?

CHAPTER 1

Misery Always Waiting

In 1988 I was eleven years old. Eleven years old with a flock of butterflies fluttering in my stomach. Sometimes boiling acid. I was a worried soul.

What should I do?

How do I escape from this perpetual agitation?

"Ahhhh, ahhhh!" always screaming from the inside. That's how it felt: *agony*. Would the agony ever heal—or would it go on forever?

I was searching for inner peace, for serenity, but it always fled, just beyond my reach, running from me. That feeling again! It would not stop!

Oh no!

Dear Big Spirit in the sky, please don't let it happen again.

Please!

I had to hide.

Father in Heaven, God (that is what my Mommy calls you), can you make me disappear? *Please?*

The silence was shattered. BAM! BAM! CRASH!...the sound of pots, pans and dishes smashed and thrown to the ground.

"Nadira! Nadira!"

That was dad. He was home.

Please Father God can you save my mommy from him? Then a long, deafening silence…

Pain was in the air. Everyone could feel it. Our house of pain. Next I heard a low, scornful whimpering followed by wailing and a loud cry. An unmistakable cry of anguish and defeat.

It was Mommy, pleading desperately for mercy. It was her cry for mercy as my dad smashed her head one time then another against the kitchen's brick wall. I thought he would never stop.

Our house was about 1,000 square feet in size, with two bedrooms. There was no place to hide.

He slammed his fist into her breast, with hard, swift brutal punches. He was pummeling her body, using his fists and feet like some unstoppable motor out of control. Finally she passed out from the pain. This was a moment I would never forget.

It was an uneven match, tiny David pitted against Goliath. My six foot tall father towered over my mother, who was a good foot shorter. He weighed at least twice as much as her and along with his height and ferocity, used that to his advantage, taking my mother down.

I could ignore the evidence of my senses. Where was God? What was this called?

I remember thinking, *You must not cry. You have to be strong.* I can still hear his maddened voice echoing in my head, "YOU ARE A CURSE! I DON'T WANT SUCH A CURSE IN MY HOUSE."

I was five years old and living in a third world country; my undeveloped child's mind had no idea of what it was I supposed to do. No idea of what 'behaving' a certain way meant. Nor how these scenes of violence and battery would later impact my life. The worst moments in my life stood out most prominently, overshadowing the good ones.

Has anyone ever questioned why?

Does the pain outlast all the other feelings--or is life just set up this way?

RING, RING! RING!

Darn! It was is the phone: I must have overslept.

What time was it?

"Hello...Hi old lady." (It was grandmother, from my mother's side. I liked teasing her that way). "Why are you calling me this early," I asked, pretending to be annoyed.

"Well, I wanted to remind you that I'm coming over to get a haircut. Get to the salon before your real clients show up. Were you still asleep? My goodness, child, its almost 8 a.m."

I hesitated before responding.

"It's OK, no problem! I was having a terrible dream. Actually I'm glad you woke me up."

"Hmm," she muttered. "Still getting those nightmares? Please take my advice: get some professional help."

After a slight pause I answered.

"Yes, old lady, I've already made an appointment. For later today. Come by in a half hour so I can do your hair before my first client arrives."

"OK love," she said. "I am walking over now. I should be there soon."

My grandma now lives about five blocks away, with my aunt. She migrated here two years ago.

CHAPTER 2

Therapy

Day dreaming on the train ride to my appointment: not a good idea. Given my taste for escaping reality into fantasy, I could end up miles away before realizing I had missed my stop.

I was in my late 20's, a passenger on the 'A' train from Queens, New York. The click and static of the intercom, and the conductor's voice announcing our approaching destination, brought me back to reality. For a very brief moment I had slipped back into my make-believe world. I love it there. Make-believe Land is my only escape, the only play my soul finds peace and freedom. Peace and freedom from the deep scars, temporary respite from the pain and the unimaginable horrors of the past.

"Ma'am...ma'am?"

I was quickly brought back to reality by the sound of the receptionist's voice. She was addressing me.

"Oh, hi," I said. I managed a quick smile. "I'm here to see Dr. Irene."

"And your name?"

"It's Veemala," I answered. "Sorry, I thought I had mentioned that."

She gave me a quizzical look which made me very self-conscious. Being self-conscious was my baseline--something that I had been struggling with all of my life. Searching for my identity. The receptionist's question made me even *more* self-conscious.

"Please be seated. I'll let you know when it's your turn," she told me. She continued to give me that questionable look as I walked towards my seat. I could feel her eyes on my back.

Had to refresh my make-up before seeing the therapist. I pulled out my make-up case (something I am never without), staring at my reflection in the compact's tiny mirror. I was horrified at what I saw: long, dark streaks of mascara from my eyes, and blotches of my natural skin tone peeking through my otherwise carefully made up face.

Ha! That was my own voice, laughing at me in amusement and derision. No wonder the receptionist kept staring at me like that!

I had been so engulfed by sorrow, so overwhelmed by the past while riding the train that I did not even realize I was weeping, flooding my face with tears. After so many moments like this I firmly resolved to forgive myself for reverting back to childhood.

Oh well, too late...

"Veemala?"

I heard my name and stood up. Dr. Irene reached her hand out to welcome me.

"I am Dr. Irene. This way please."

CHAPTER 3

Conversation With Dr. Irene

The room was small, not quite how I had envisioned it. I was expecting something much larger in scale, a contemporary space replete with high ceiling, big wide windows, and low comfortable couches…Not!.

How silly of me.

From the moment I landed in the States (arriving at Miami International Airport in 2003) I felt I had touched down in a day dream, in a (good) fantasy land filled with bright lights, towering skyscrapers, millions of cars, busses, trains and planes.

This land was waiting to embrace me. It freed me from the dark clutches of violent savagery and trembling fear of the people and country I once knew.

"I see you were referred by Dr. Zhao?" she asked. "And what kind of treatment do you think you need?"

Suddenly I was drawn back from my dark thoughts to the miraculous present.

"What? Oh, I'm sorry," I apologized. Would there ever come a time when I didn't need to instinctively *apologize*? "Well, Dr. Zhao feels that I should get help for all the things that have affected my life. You see, I'm not who you think I am... but I am really me." I offered what seemed like confused words by way of explanation.

The words flowed from my mouth like water from a burst dam.

"I have two brothers and one sister. I am the oldest. I am originally from Guyana, which is the only English-speaking country in South America. My country had been colonized by the British and my ancestors came there from India.

"They were brought there as indentured slaves, along with Africans, Chinese, Amerindians, Portuguese and Europeans. Guyana gained its independence in 1966 and ever since the country has had massive political problems."

I wanted to yell out to the world, wanted everyone to know about all the indignities and violence I had endured in forced silence for so many years...but Dr. Irene gently placed her hands on my shoulder, stopping me in mid-sentence.

"Veemala," she said. "It's alright. Let me explain how it works. Much as you might want to, you can't cover 30 years of life experience in one 30 minute sitting! Suppose we set you up with a schedule of some 30 minute sessions for three weeks or so. At that point, with a better idea of your issues, we will re-evaluate the situation, perhaps set you up with psychiatrist. Would you like something to drink?"

I shook my head, *No,* and she suggested that I get a little more comfortable. She indicated another chair that was wider and lower, right beside the gentle muted light of a small table lamp.

I welcomed the suggestion. It was a great one. I felt comfortable and protected, as though I were in a cocoon.

Dr. Irene offered some warm tea, which I gladly accepted. It tasted great--almost soothing!

Dr. Irene ignored the rapid knocking on the door. She simply didn't respond. Then the phone rang. She answered it.

Shortly after this she left the room but quickly returned, taking a package from her desk as she apologized, asking me to make myself comfortable. She would be back shortly.

I felt so comfortable. so protected... soon enough I drifted into a light doze. Hmm...This was good. *I needed this.*

I had not felt this way since--ever. It was a sweet moment and I lingered there. *Being in the moment...*like sitting on a beach caressed by a soft summer breeze.

CHAPTER 4

Seeking A Savior

At age 10--yes, I am 10 years old now, but was there any difference from five years before?

Nothing had changed. It all felt the same.

The only thing that changed was the day; nothing different in the moment, nothing in the action of the others around me.

If only they would let me play with them, like all the other children do. If only I could walk or run to places like others do. If only my brain could figure a way out, how to fix things, how to convince them, how to explain it all.

Imagine waking up every day in a prison. A prison with no guards, no parole and no release date. There is just one inmate – you.

The prison? My body was the prison, trapping the real me inside. The me I desperately wanted to be but could not. Whenever I tried to get out the others would push me back in, or attack me for being different.

No love for me inside this prison without walls, and no love for me at home.

If only love could live in our house.

What if love did live in our house? Would life be any better? Would it?

"Vishal! And Veemala! Come on, hurry up, we have to run! He is going to kill us!"

I hear the sharpening of the machete. I hear him say it.

"Tonight I'm going to slice you up into pieces."

Why was my dad doing this, threatening to cut my mummy up into pieces?

Why?

"Dear God..."

Oh yes, now that I am older, I know His name. At five years old I thought of him as the Great Spirit in the sky. My mother had a different name for him: our loving Father God.

Odd, how I am able to process all of this in one frightening moment. Why is my mind constantly on a roll? Why the constant rain in my heart?

I envisioned a future of mindlessly repeating every action, every terror-soaked gesture, that my mom performed with well-practiced ease. My life seemed hellbent toward a depressive frenzy.

In my opinion, no child should have to see or hear such things. No wonder the world is the way it is today; no wonder the high rates of child suicide. Why should any child be driven to destroy him-or herself?

There is terror, and cruelty and evil in this world. Some speculate that somehow, someday, a change will come. But they are ultimately more concerned with the 'real' issues: the bills they have to pay, the anger that screams for release, the thirst for alcohol: not the hearts of the little ones…a little one like me.

My brother and I were left out, excluded. We might as well have been invisible. Saying those prayers was my only outlet. Over time they grew old, like all things in life, and still we needed to be saved.

CHAPTER 5

A Small Step Towards Freedom

It was just past 8 a.m. and my mother gently woke me and my brother. Mom was thin and petitie, with long lustrous brown hair. My brother was a year younger than me and very brave for his age.

"It's time to go back to the house and pack our things," our mom said. "Your father has already left for work and that gives us enough time to get out. We are going to stay with your grandmother."

We were seeking shelter at our mother's mother. I still hear the sounds from last night, my father sharpening the machete and threatening our mother's life.

By now our neighbors were all accustomed to hearing the screams of agony that habitually came from our house. They were well aware of the brutal beatings our mother had to endure at the hands of our alcoholic father.

Why didn't anyone say something? Or call for help? Why didn't anyone step in?

They could have easily intervened--there were dozens if not hundreds of opportunities. Anyone could have called someone for help...but no one did. We always had to go to them, pleading for refuge.

Spending the night at the neighbor's, hiding from our father's alcohol-fueled rage, became the norm.

My mother thanked our neighbor for the shelter we received and we walked hurriedly back towards our small house. They knew what was happening but all they did was help us to hide.

I guess that was better than nothing.

I am so excited that we would not be coming back to this house, a house full of distress, a house that cries and groans...just like my mommy does when her head is being beaten into the wall by my dad.

"Oh God! Please stop those horrible sounds from echoing in my head."

The slaps, punches and beatings I witnessed have been eating away at my brain. The sight of my poor mother's limp body has become a torment to my soul...

"Vemeela!"

I hear my younger brother calling me as I stand daydreaming in the hallway of our house. I was, for a moment, excited: finally we were leaving, running away from daddy. But I am sad, too.

Why do I feel sad? For whom am I sad? I had no friends. That's right:

NO FRIENDS, not in my small neighborhood and most definitely not at school.

I was about to walk pass the spot in the living room where my dad usually sat when I suddenly froze.

"No! No!" I cried out loud, as I placed my unusually small hands over my ears to try and block out the thought that was crossing my mind. *It's true, it's all true, but why do I want to block it out?* How could I have forgotten this? How?

Only old people forget things, not young ones like me. That is what mom always said.

The vision in my head was vivid. I saw my dad hugging me tightly, tears flooding his eyes and streaming down his face. The words he spoke touched me. His words touch me even now as I reflect back on that scene in my head. My dad loves me, yes, he truly loves. Why am I sure?

Because he said it to me.

Yes, my dad cried and said that he truly loves me. Why did I not remember that? Why?

I love my dad, too.

But why am I invisible to him when there are friends and family around? Why?

Once again my brother's voice interrupted my thoughts, moving me to action.

"Veemala, Ma wants us to help her pack," he said. "Hurry up."

"I'm coming, I'm coming! Stop calling me," I shouted back to him, upset that he had disturbed my daydream.

CHAPTER 6

We Move In

Arriving at my grandmother's house that day was a big relief for me.

No more unjustified beatings from my father--are beatings ever justified?--and the end of my mother running and hiding in fear. No longer do I have to watch in horror as my brave younger brother tries to step in and stop the beatings.

I was released from the prison that was my father's house. No longer would I have to cower away from the sad disdainful stares from the man I called Daddy. I was safe now.

Was I?

I stood in my grandmother's house listening to the chatter of the older family members, who were talking excitedly about our arrival, planning who was going to sleep where. My grandmother did not live alone. Another of her six daughters and her family--my aunt, her husband and their two children--lived there too. These cousins were around the same age as my brother and me.

The whole clan living in a small, three bedroom house. I knew that things were going to be much different from usual, but I didn't know how.

I didn't fully understand it but my heart felt lighter, some of the weight of the sorrow and fear of our own house lifted. Blessed relief! Now my mom would smile--smile at me--more.

I was so happy! I loved when my mom hugged and comforted me. I felt like nothing could harm me, with my brave mother, my brave mother hen protecting her young.

I craved that love each moment of my life. And who would not?

I wished moments like those would spring up like blooming flowers, regularly, predictably, forever…but my daydreams, my fantasy world, was too often unrealizable, unrealistic. Clinging to dreams that might never come true was a regular habit of mine.

Dad, oh Dad!

I was hoping a day would arrive when he would turn over a new leaf and we would have a normal happy family. Decency and order would preside… but that was just another impossible dream.

We were like runaway slaves, having to escape from our own father. I am sure mother thanked God for this respite from hopelessness and from the nights of beatings.

Staying one day longer could have ended her life.

It is 1989. We had been living with grandmother and my cousins for a year. I was 11 years old.

All of us lived together under one roof; most of our belongings remained packed and there was no privacy. My grandmother's house was located in the county of Essequibo, an agricultural area that was also home to our country's largest river. We lived on top of one another; having enough money, having food to eat, were my mother's greatest worries. She needed to feed us and provide our material needs for us though she had never worked outside the home. We lived on the pittance doled out to her by my dad on an irregular, infrequent basis. My dad spent most of his money on drink. We were free from dad's physical and emotional abuse but we suffered terribly from financial privation. It was nearly impossible to get by.

Living in this overcrowded, underfed household was becoming unbearable. My mother looked for work.

Guyana was mostly wilderness. The water supply was affected by the sewage and toxic chemicals spewing forth from the factories.

Guyana sits on the northeast coach of South America, close to the Caribbean Sea. Venezuela, Brazil and Surinam are its neighbors.

Most of Guyana's population were poor--just like us. Guyana, a third world country, was ranked the poorest in all of South America.

You can see and read about the struggle my mother and those around us went through. In a *Travel GC* article one author described our country like this: Crime is prevalent across Guyana. Assaults, break-ins, armed robberies, pickpocketing, purse snatching, theft from cars and carjacking are all common. Be particularly cautious in the Georgetown areas of Stabroek Market, Tiger Bay and south of Brickdam Street. Criminals prefer to target foreigners and returning Guyanese citizens.

Sadly enough, his observations were true. Only the strong survive in Guyana; I attribute my survival to sheer luck. We were not the only family struggling to stay alive. Other children walked the streets too.

There were no safe places for children in Guyana--especially for a child like me.

CHAPTER 7

School Of Hard Knocks

How slowly a year goes by when the one person you love and rely on exits your world. No reason, no excuse in the world was justification enough to soothe my pain, not even the fact that we had saved my mom from my drunken homicidal dad.

One year in my life felt like a million. I was in a torture cell filled with nails and thorns, built for me alone. I was terrified that I would stop breathing, so I could almost never fall asleep. I dreaded the dreams and nightmares that exploded every night in my brain.

The single exception was school. I loved school. I wanted to learn and fit in. Unfortunately none of that was in the cards. Life chose a very different path for me.

Mom finally found a job--living as a nanny--in Venezuela. The boat she will travel on leaves tomorrow morning, at 6:45 a.m. Which meant she would be leaving my grandmother's house at four. Another piece of my life slipping from the pitiful grasp of our hands.

We would have to raise ourselves.

I see myself, head is spinning, unable to contain my tears. I am on the receiving end of nasty stares and rude suggestions from the rest of the family.

"Shut up!" they yell. "Stop crying!"

"You need to be brave now," they said later. My inner self screamed for help.

"Veemala, can you take me back to where you said your dad never wanted to give you attention when the rest of the family or friends were around?"

"Veemala...are you awake? Veemala?"

What?

I must have fallen asleep. I didn't hear Dr. Irene entering the room.

What was she saying?

How embarrassing. How long had I been sleeping?

What should my answer be?

"I am dreadfully sorry Doctor, I must have dozed off," I said. "If you could tell me where you buy that tea I just drank I'm sure my nights would be much more bearable."

I was rambling practically babbling, afraid to stop talking. Afraid I might have said something embarrassing while asleep.

Wait a minute...that's why I'm here...to get some help, some relief from the nightmares...

Overthinking, endless worry, was my daily tonic. Clearly it was showing. *OK Veemala, relax. Nothing to fear here*, I told myself. I just couldn't help viewing everything in my life as worthless, unlovable, dejected and lost.

"You were asleep for a good part of the hour but you have shared quite a bit," Dr. Irene explained. "You are so filled with pain that each time you close your eyes, your mouth opens up, and some of that pain comes spilling out."

I sat staring at the kind doctor, wondering how much I might have said.

"We will begin where we left off, same time next week, OK?" she remarked. "Oh, would you like to take home a few packets of that tea?"

I accepted the offer gladly. I might even get decent night's sleep.

Walking to the train station I felt some relief: a slight reprieve, which was a blessing, some respite from the tension and hurt I always feel. Usually I have an uncomfortable feeling in my chest.

No doubt about it: sharing is good.

Tea in hand, I boarded the train for Queens. Destination: home.

Who can foresee the future? Who could imagine the infinite fear I am about to disclose?

CHAPTER 8

Farewell, Mother

"I am only doing this to make life better for you and your brother," my mother explained. "I won't be gone for long. You see how hard life is for us like this? I love you and your brother very much. It won't be long, just a couple of months, OK?"

My mother's voice kept playing in my head: "I love you, I will be back soon."

Her words painted the walls of my ears.

Then it was morning, much too soon.

She hugged us, told us to behave, and repeated that she loved us. I cried uncontrollably.

My brother cried, too, but not the way I did. He was always in better control of his emotions. It had not been a full three hours since our mother had gone that my life became a downwards spiral towards a destiny I did not choose, a destiny brutally forced upon me.

This house had become another prison--just like like my father's house before. Granted there was no Goliath threatening to crush us, but now, without my mother, was nobody to care for us. My brother and I would be treated like servants, unloved lackeys of my aunt and uncle. And there was nothing we could do about it.

"Veemala!"

Hearing my name in this new empty hell sent shivers down my spine. The sadness of my mother's departure weighed heavily on my heart and soul.

"Coming," was my weak response. Sheer pressure made it difficult to speak.

I kept replaying the words of a sad song in my head –'*When will I see you again, Will I have to suffer and struggle forever?'*

I made up some of the words but it was my song. My private song of pain.

As I wiped at my tear-stained face I prepared myself for what was to come. My aunt stood by the back door watching me as I emerged from the outdoor toilet. The latrine. The latrine, became the crying place for my overburdened heart.

"Child, hurry up! Almost seven o'clock and you need to take the cows and goats out to pasture." The pasture was about a half mile from the house.

"When you are done you will need to wash out these diapers and hang them on the line. And don't let them touch the ground! Hurry, if you want to go to school..."

My heart skipped several beats. *Why, why, why?*

"Yes auntie, I'm coming."

I was never afraid of animals, and it was quite easy for me to lead the cows and goats to pasture. At first I was even excited about being in control of *something* in my life. But after the first two or three days of trudging through slushy mud and cow manure it got old really fast. The chores got to me in the worst possible way.

It was exhausting running after the cows and goats as I tried to bring them in line with the rest of the herd. On many occasions one or more of them took off in different directions--usually in opposite directions--and then I'd be late for school.

I was always late for school.

I can barely recall what I ate for breakfast. A quick grab at a cup of black tea and a small bun or a slice of buttered bread was my portion. I dared not ask for more.

That is how I came to feel. When the hunger pangs hit me hard, I kept thinking about my mom, about how much she loved me. There was enough food--enough food for all--just not for me.

I watched my cousins stuff their faces. I watched as they tossed their leftovers to the dogs and chickens in the yard. I watched as auntie Bee and her husband spoiled my cousins with love.

They got everything they asked for--and then some. They played for long hours outdoors with their friends. They were encouraged to get their school work done before bed. They got to choose the best fruits and enjoyed the comfort of their beds. Not me! I had to sleep on the floor. I never had free time to recover from the hard days of many unreasonable chores. Fun or enjoyment were completely out of the question.

Hugs and kisses were necessities I could only dream of. I watched with envy as my cousins were showered with hugs and kisses, with embraces from my grandmother and their parents. The only time I ever got them were in fantasies.

I daydream a lot.

I daydream while walking the cattle to and from the pasture. I daydream on my way to school and in I daydream in school.

Such dreams! I see myself in beautiful clothing, in ball rooms, moving graciously and being admired by elegant men and women. There are times when I could almost taste the rich, decadent meals piled high on large oaken tables.

In my head I am complete and happy--almost euphoric. Without these fantasies I have nothing. I am nothing.

I feel so alone. I have a brother and but my mom is in another country, very far away. Oh, I almost forgot. I have a dad.

I still feel like a motherless child: yes, an orphan.

I think it might rain. I hate when the clouds are dark and unrevealing, but the rain I love. Walking in the rain with my thoughts and fantasies, no one to disturb or distract me from fantasies that only I could dream of...and hope would one day come true.

Standing behind my grandmother I feel the darkness of the clouds entering my soul. It gives me chills, gives me feelings I have never had before.

Suddenly a loud boom.: the sound of thunder, from which I recoil in fear.

Simultaneously I heard auntie's husband telling me to go outside.

"Get the animals! It's going to rain hard and I don't want them to get soaked."

Then he walks away.

CHAPTER 9

The Beginning Of
Many Storms

It was dark, wet and cold as I hurried along the narrow, uneven path towards the pasture for the animals. Today was very different. I could feel it in my bones, the fear of what lay ahead. That day I learned that my gut feeling, my intuition were never wrong.

But I had to do my chores.

So off I went. I entered the pasture about 50 yards or so from the field where the cows and goats were moving restlessly. That's when I saw a dark shadow emerging from the cover of a shaded tree.

Who was there?

It was too early, still too dark and wet for anyone to be out here--except me, of course. The shadow was approaching me and I felt my throat go dry. Waves of nervous heat radiated from my forehead. Even in the cold and rain I could still feel the heat.

I was paralyzed with fear, trying to think of some way to protect myself, but I was so frightened that I could not think straight.

The shadow spoke. "I know what you are," he said, as he moved closer and closer toward me.

"And I want some sex."

My voice sounded like someone else's voice, echoing from very far away.

"No, no, leave me alone," I pleaded.

But I was weak from fear and my throat was parched. If only someone would come along and save me, just show up and interrupt this nightmare.

Suddenly, his hands were on my body. I struggled to back away from him, trying my best to shout or scream.

But no sound came from my desert dry throat. I was paralyzed by fear.

The monster slammed my frail body against a tree, his arms locked tight around me. I was small and frail and he had me in his grip. (After moving to my grandmother's house my physical appearance and mental stability declined. I was now a very skinny, fragile child, thanks to the extremely hard daily labor and the meagre portions of food thrown my way.

Malnourished, deprived of all human affection, I looked different: an outcast, some kind of alien or freak.

I tried to fight but I was no match for that man, the monster who was attacking me, taking me down. He molested me, his rough, gnarled fingers ripping into my flesh, choking my neck as he forced his hands down between my legs to paw at my privates.

It was then that he began to grunt, nearly incomprehensible barks and commands.

"I KNOW YOU WANT IT. TAKE IT. TELL ME HOW MUCH YOU NEED IT; OH YES TELL ME. TAKE IT. LET ME GIVE IT TO YOU GOOD. DON'T FIGHT BACK BECAUSE NO ONE IS HERE BUT US…"

As he slammed my slight body to the ground as my mind floated in the air somewhere above me. It watched with horror as the monster attacked me in the most shocking and gruesome way possible.

He tugged, dragged and ripped my clothes from my body as I begged and pleaded for him to stop. I knew the whole time that it was hopeless. The ground was hard and cruel against my flesh, like the nasty, soulless man forcing me down. His weight on top of me made it impossible to escape.

He penetrated me. The sudden shocking pain, the assault on my body and private parts were like death to me. He ravaged my anus and I prayed to die.

I prayed to die; prayed for the earth to open and swallow me up. That would have been best. He slammed himself into my body repeatedly, thrusting in and out again and again, deeper and harder.

At some point I must have passed out from the combined terror and pain. The sexual assault was ferocious, bestial…when I did wake this predator was violating my innards with his massive member. I was darting in and out of consciousness but then noticed through my tears a second figure looming over us.

It was another man.

I felt a flicker of hope--was someone was there to save me?--but no, I was so wrong.

I quickly spotted the unnatural, strange excitement in the eyes of this stranger and I knew…life for me was over. My frail body would be unable to endure a double assault.

The stranger spoke to my assailant.

"You know, I have to get a turn too, if I'm not going to tell," he glibly joked with my attacker.

I could see the dark sky, the rain blinding my tear-filled eyes. The trees were shook with the wind blowing in hatred towards the earth. The earth upon which I was brutally raped.

My assailant pulled out of my body and laughed.

"Sure man, go ahead, take your turn," he said to the newcomer. "It's going to be our little secret."

My mind went blank and my body numb. I must have died for an hour--that's how or it felt. I regained consciousness to find both my assailants standing there smiling at each other.

I struggled to put my clothes on as they helped me. I blurted out that I was going to tell my family.

But that only made them laugh hysterically.

"Go ahead, no one will believe you," one of them said to me, laughing more uproariously. "And if you do then everyone will know what you are, and you will bring shame on yourself and your family."

As they walked away I could hear them laughing--like two pals sharing a good joke--and I saw them threatening and sneering at me. They were two cousins who lived four houses away from us. They were supposed to be decent Christian boys, upstanding models for the community--but they sure proved how indecent and irreligious they were.

They were in their early twenties, about 5 feet 10 inches tall; they sang in the church choir and assisted with baptisms in the local Christian church. It was going to be my word against theirs; who would protect me anyway? All I could focus on was death. I wanted to die, wanted the earth to burst and take me down.

I cannot recall how I got back home but I do recall that aunt demanding explanations from me. Why I was late? How my clothes became torn? It was dark and wet and stormy; the power and lights were out. In the darkness, still in a daze, I considered a dozen possible explanations. Finally I told them that I fell, that my clothes got caught on the pasture's barbed wire fence while getting one of the cows out from the mud in the pasture.

I guess that was reason enough for her, and so ended our conversation.

That night I fell asleep wracked with pain and sorrow. All I wanted was for the earth to burst open and swallow me up. I had been raped and there was no one to protect me. It hurts.

What would anyone do if I actually talked about it? No one would believe me. They would just laugh. Especially since I walked, talked and even acted differently beyond my control.

Our neighbor's son and his cousin had raped me: teenage boys from a strong religious background. I decided to stay quiet and keep it all to myself: *my little secret.*

My brother went back to live with my daddy. Now I was completely alone, amidst the circle of my uncaring family. My dad had came back to take me but my aunt and grandmother convinced him to let me stay with them since I would get a better education. So he left.

My life was useless, ruined. I could not think of anything or anyone; I could not think. I was completely numb, completely oblivious to the people and the world around me--an orphans who craved and cried daily for her mother's return. All I had and lived by was hope.

Two days later it happened again. My two nemeses, my two rapists were there waiting for me in the pasture.

There was no place to run, nowhere to hide, just a wide open field, the animals my only witnesses. It was time for my mind and soul to escape, to run for cover to their private hiding place, a place without pain, a place where I could never be found. A place detached from my body, the body that belonged to everyone but me.

So began the almost daily cycle of rape and assault on my body by these two soulless monsters. As time went by so did the men, from one attacker to another, from one rapist to another.

I started to want it, to welcome my daily violation. I became accustomed to the brutal sex; I actually felt that somehow it healed my pain and sorrow. Many times I even told my attacker that I would be waiting for him there in the pasture.

I created countless fantasies in my head, fantasies that kept me distracted from the curses that plagued my life. The fantasies also served as distraction from my many chores, chores that began at 5:30 a.m. and ended late into the night. Each night I laid my weary head down on the hard pillow and collapsed onto the 1-inch mattress they had provided for me on the floor--always on the floor. The only way I could fall asleep was imagining that my mother was there, hugging me and rocking me to sleep. Meanwhile hordes of mosquitoes bit away at me.

My aunt and the rest of the relatives thought little of it, but my daily 'chores' were nothing but child labor from the perspective of the normal world. I always hoped that I would be in a higher and better place in the future: anywhere better and higher. Those were my hopes that I lived by. Many days I was in my trance, mesmerized by my dreams of power. Being famous was my greatest dream.

CHAPTER 10

A Childhood Robbed

My nights were long and sleepless, filled with fears and flashbacks of what I had experienced throughout the day, the week--throughout my whole miserable existence.

I usually woke to the crowing of the cock. It is 5:30 a.m.--time to rise up and fold up my sleeping items from the floor.

I hear movement in my aunt's room so I hurry to avoid her scalding accusations that I am late, that I am dragging my feet.

First thing to do is let the chickens out, a process far more demanding than any desk job could ever be. Farm work is hard work. So is getting along with cows, goats and chickens without getting harmed. I would scatter the chicken feed on the ground and fill their trays with water.

The pasture where I take the cows and goats is about a half mile away. I have to move quickly--it can take quite a bit of time getting them there. Animals are strange--they don't t always cooperate! They don't always move along at the pace you would like. Most times it takes a lot of effort prodding them along while keeping an eye on the goats so they don't stray far from the flock.

Some of the cows had to be tethered to a post that was shaded or close to water. In today's society nobody would dare do such a thing.

I had a great deal agricultural experience so being around those animals was like being among friends. Once I was done it usually took a full 20 minutes to return home.

Immediately upon my return I would have to sweep beneath the house. Unlike here in America, homes in my country are built on stilts that raise them above ground--the ground bare dirt, not concrete. It was my job to keep it clean, which meant sweeping it at least twice a day.

Even today Guyana still needs major improvements. The country still faces major issues. I would like to be a positive influence, to make things better there, especially for its children. Many live in poverty and in poor housing conditions, even as I write this.

One positive note: the government is finally beginning to focus on the poor. Country housing developments are in the works and investments into Guyanese communities are being actively encouraged.

Then my grandmother brought a baby cousin home. One of my other aunts gave birth to this cute little baby boy whom my grandmother was now going to raise.

Everyday there were eight or more diapers to be washed, and as usual, the task fell to me. Washing diapers was very time consuming; they had be free of any stains. I had that job for about nine months.

Every day I hear the same thing from my aunt or my grandmother as I wash them.

"You need to hurry up with the washing," and "Make sure you get all the stains out, don't hang them too low on the clothesline."

This was my life, and in life you have to take things as they are. The family was the priority and grandma made sure to keep everyone in order. Especially before we headed for school.

School starts at 8 a.m. and I am taking a shower outside, in the back yard. I quickly swallow the slice of unbuttered bread or pancake, chasing it down with a cold up of tea or coffee. I grab my school bag and start running along the unpaved street to my school.

School was also about a half mile from home so it took some time to get there. I always barely make it to class but many days I am late, coming in just as the other kids are about to start writing in their books.

Once there, I find I am breathing hard, trying to recover from the morning chores and all the hassles of the day. Teachers whipped students who were late; I usually got two lashes in the outstretched palms of my hand whenever I was late, which was almost every day-- but I was used to it.

I loved school but the other kids didn't love me. They made it very hard for me. I was teased and bullied and called every ugly word in the book. Processing information was difficult for me because my memory was shot.

I succeeded in school by sheer will power and the grace of the Lord above.

On my way home from school, I always had confusing thoughts. For example, I wondered if I should hurry home to avoid all of the hardcore teasing, tugging and pushing I had to endure from my peers- -or should I drag it out, and walk slowly, so I would not have to face the huge amount of work waiting for me at home?

But I had no way of avoiding that. No matter how late I arrived home, I had no choice but to do them. Always foremost in my mind was the daily rape by those monsters waiting to ambush me in the pasture.

With all these thoughts swirling in my brain I finally arrived home from school. After dropping my school bag in a corner and changing into what we call "house clothes" I headed down to my aunt and uncle's farm.

The farm was almost a mile from home; a half mile beyond the pasture. I always had various things to do depending on the day of the week and on what my uncle had in mind for me that particular day. There was always something to do; I had fetch firewood, and had to clean the trench and pond.

Today was weeding day. I hacked at the weeds and shrubs with a machete. There were many, very overgrown, and they had to be cleared away. I found a batch of little plants placed there by my uncle to remind me to replant them in the same plot I chopped the weeds.

I was standing, looking at the small plants I had just put in the earth. I was hoping for some time to breathe, for a break from the intense work under the harsh sun, when I heard the screech of my uncle's voice.

"Don't just stand there wasting time, you have to water the plants!" he screamed. "Otherwise they will die! Get the bucket, fetch some water from the pond and start wetting them. Now! After that I need you to dig four holes along the fence line. Tomorrow I am going to run barbed wires to keep out the animals."

I hurried away to do as he asked; I did not want to be there alone in the dark. I still had to drive the cows and goats home from the pasture. He was inhuman and heartless--he always treated me so bad.

I am so tired. This is such hard work. Then there was the homework I needed to get done...

I need the strength of a man--three men!--to complete these tasks. But my body was only equipped for a woman's work--one woman.

It is 7 p.m. and I am making my way home, a large bunch of bananas on my head. It feels like 50 pounds but it may only be 25; a jute bag hung from my shoulder, crammed with vegetables my uncle wanted me to take back home.

I could barely move with all this weight but I had to hurry: I still had to get the cattle from the pasture. On tiring days like these I hope and pray that my attackers are not there. Sometimes I actually wanted them to be there so I could feel numb.

On that particular day I had given up all hope. I didn't even want the attackers to be there. But yes, there they were, ready to pounce.

I am finally home from the pasture with the cattle broken, battered and dazed from what my abusers have once again inflicted upon me. It would be a blessing to die now. Nothing in this world will ever bring me joy. Amen.

Faint and practically lifeless, I slowly walked to the chicken coup and leaned my head against the frame. I walked around the coop with a flashlight, counting the chickens to be sure that they were all there.

After that I forced my arms above my head in order to pour water on my bruised limbs. I wept. I then moved slowly up the back stairs of the house and made my way to the kitchen table where my small portion of curry and rice was left waiting for me.

I was starving but I could not eat; all I could think about was my mother. Where was she? Why wasn't she here? I felt so empty inside, so deprived of my brother, my daddy and of course my mom.

Oh how I missed them!

9 p.m.: I can finally lay my head down on the hard, lumpy pillow. But wait! First I must get some coconut oil to rub my great-grandmother's feet.

Yes, I forgot to mention that my great grandmother was alive and she too lived in that small house. Rubbing the soles of her feet each night was a ritual I did not mind--she cared about me and wished me no harm and assured me that some day all my suffering would come to an end.

She was 78 years old and she had neither the strength nor the power to protect me. The house we all lived still belonged to her. She told me stories of the hard work of her younger years and how her mom was actually born during their ocean passage from India to Guyana...and there was more.

It was time to close my eyes and hope for some sleep. I closed my eyes on another full day of hard labor and rape.

"Good night, Veemala. Try to get some rest."

That was my great-grandmother trying to comfort me, ignorant of my trials but possessing the wisdom and love to comfort me nonetheless.

CHAPTER 11

Therapist – Second Visit

The train ride from Jamaica, Queens to downtown Manhattan is always an adventure for me. It allows me to sit back and observe the constant movement of people, people of all nationalities and cultures.

New York, the greatest melting pot in the world.

I analyze everyone that passes by, everyone standing there before me. As they turn to disembark, I wonder if *anyone* shared the same issues and miseries I had borne.

I tried to read their thoughts and envisioned how they handled their mishaps. You see many different faces in New York; sometimes the same, sometimes new ones. Everyone looks different and you can tell most are in their own world while *en route*.

I truly admire every face I see, everyone skin color, shape and size. Somehow it all makes me feel connected and relevant. I feel relaxed on the train. I have no worries. I can take one breathe at a time.

My turn to step off the train. I arrive at West 4th Street at 3:39 p.m. My appointment with Dr. Irene is in six minutes; I hope I am not late.

It makes me anxious: I still have four long blocks to walk. As soon I step off the train I see the hustle and bustle in the street,.packed with people going to and fro.

Unlike Guyana, jobs are easier to find here and it is easier to learn a trade. My life had turned into The Great American Dream...well, sort of...

"Hi Veemala. Dr. Irene asked that I show you to her waiting room. She apologizes for running a bit late--an emergency visit to another client," the receptionist said.

Whew!! I was so relieved--but then I saw a hulking mass of a man, another patient emerging from the other doctor's office there. He looked exactly like one of my attackers. I started to get scared and shake but managed to convince that this was a different time and place and I could safely wait for Dr. Irene.

"I think I'll just sit in the same comfortable chair I sat in last time," I said.

There was coffee brewing and a tea pot full of hot water. Next to it was a box containing a colorful assortment of teas.

"Help yourself," said the receptionist.

After fixing myself a cup of herbal tea I chose what is now my favorite reclining chair. As my eyes roamed around the room I tried to find Dr. Irene's personality in the furnishings, in some of the paintings on the walls. I wanted to know how her journey into psychology began. I wondered what her success rate was with people like me.

I wondered if she could actually help me make the journey back from hell,

Through the drawn drapery I could see the darkening sky. The clouds were settled into each other, creating a dark dense shadow.

My body slid deeper into the embrace of the reclining chair.

CHAPTER 12

Deja Vu

My memory is rushing backwards: it is a Sunday afternoon in May, 1993, when I was 15 years old. Just like today it started out with bright sunshine and cool wind as the preacher's words of hope and wisdom lingered in my head.

I have just attended a church service and made my way home, where I now resided with my father, clueless as to what awaited me there.

Suddenly, the clouds darkened with the sound of thunder. Flashes of lighting lit up the sky.

I hastened home, hoping to to avoid the imminent deluge of rain. Somewhere in my head I kept hearing the words: "It takes more courage to reveal insecurities than to hide them, more strength to relate to people than to dominate them, more manhood to abide by thought out principles than by blind reflex."

That was a quote from my pastor…or did I read it in some book? I wasn't sure, but it lifted my spirits and gave me some hope.

I moved to my father's house when the abuse and torture I suffered in grandmother's town became too much to bear. We had not heard from my mother. The only other option was returning to my father.

I was back in the very same prison as before.

Inside the house daddy was in a state of intoxicated recklessness.

One day as I stepped through the door I was literally ambushed. My father came at me with an onslaught of vicious slaps and punches. Nothing had changed, The beating would not stop until we all got away.

He lifted me up in the air and viciously slammed me to the ground. My vision fragmented, a kaleidoscope of colors from the vibrating pain in my body. I lay there helpless, listening to the worst denigrating insults spewing from his mouth.

My father considered me worthless, inept, a scourge to the family and deliberately dysfunctional. Life had become so unbearable at my grandmother's that I had returned to my father. This is what I came home to.

His painful words paralyzed me, choked me, stopping my breath. I had grown accustomed to most of the curses and insults, but today, we reached a new depth when my father said, "SOMETIMES I WISH THAT YOU WERE NEVER BORN."

The worst thing a parent could ever say. His words rang in my ears, adding new agony, a new scar to my transfixed heart.

My life was a mess and clearly needed fixing.

I wondered if any other child's life had been as shattered as mine. My head was spinning. I tottered on the brink of a bottomless chasm. Where was the remorse in my life?

I imagined I had not suffered as greatly as my mother, yet we faced the very same demon. Wounds that would fester for the rest of my life. Entire days spent trying to suppress--to erase--my feelings. An impossible task. In spite of his drinking and abuse, he always made sure that my brother and I had dinner. But his words, whether from anger or ignorance, kept spinning in my head. I wasn't needed in this world anymore. Why was I still here? Why was I fighting to live, and for whom? What was the purpose of it all, anyway?

CHAPTER 13

Death As Sanctuary

You cannot stop the rush of pain as it wells up from deep inside, inflicted by someone--my father--who would just as soon see me dead.

I started to believe this would be preferable--that it would be better if I wasn't not here at at all. If I could just vanish. Once I was gone my family would no longer have to deal with me or who I was.

From the beginning they all knew what was wrong with me. What didn't I understand?

The physical, emotional, psychological and mental pain I experienced from this latest beating at the hands of my father left me broken and numb.

The pain was still there but I could no longer feel it. Knowing that my father wished that I had never born destroyed my soul. I needed to rest, rest, rest forever in an unending sleep.

As I sat outside beneath the mango tree in the backyard of his home my thoughts ceased. I was unable to make plans, figure out what to do or where to go next. Death was welcoming to me; maybe I would find sanctuary there. I no longer cared if I lived or died.

I reached for the three bottles sitting in the corner of the small, makeshift shed.

I had often thought of suicide but could never find the strength or will power to go through with it. I thought of burning myself while at my grandmother's house but I held back because I thought things would improve sooner or later.

Now it was time.

CHAPTER 14

And On The Fourth Day...

Blackout, lost time: the four days I spent not knowing; of ceasing to exist.

Somehow I am still alive.

I was in that hospital for four days following my suicide attempt-- but still not dead.

This had to be a sign.

I had to find a way to help others, had to search for the flickering precious spirit that remained lit despite my tormented life. I had been put on Earth for a reason; the challenge was to discover what that reason was.

I was discharged from the Georgetown hospital in Guyana after a week. I returned back home to my father, stepmother and brother.

Everyone in the village knew about my suicide attempt. Understandably I was not keen on leaving the house. My villagers christened me with a new name, Grammaxone, the weed killer (poison) that I drank along with kerosene oil and detergent, to try to end my life.

I heard someone talking. It sounded like that of Dr. Irene.

"Nurse, how long has she been waiting?"

"Almost forty-five minutes."

"I totally forgot about her. Please, can you wake her and try to reschedule?"

On my way home I felt extremely drained--as if I had actually gone through a therapy session. A tub of rum raisin ice cream, two slabs of chocolate and some Indian stringy chips topped off my day.

CHAPTER 15

Holy Intervention

It was a bright, sunny Sunday in November, 1993, the same year I consumed poison and attempted suicide.

Despite that I felt very good. Going to church gave me hope. It was much needed respite from the constant fear, fear of torture and physical abuse.

I am Hindu by birth but I felt more comfortable in the Christian church, where I felt welcome and less judged. It is 9:45 that morning and so I would get to the choir and sing and hear the sermon on time. My walk to church takes only five to seven minutes.

I was about fifty yards from the church when I saw three men rushing out of the liquor shop across the street.

I ran as fast as my slender legs would carry me. Not fast enough to escape the unprovoked attack by the three men. Soon I felt the beer drenching my head and shoulders, followed by the outrageous sensation of my clothes being pulled off.

Simply because I am just me…and what is 'Wrong' with me?

These men as they lived in my village and belonged to some of the groups that verbally abused me with obscenities, threats, and invective. They were my tormentors, jailers that roamed the streets of my neighborhood.

Their greatest thrill in life was to plague me.

I tried to escape, to reach my destination—the church—but it was futile. I could not have fought back since they were stronger, heavier and taller than me. To fight or defend myself was not in my DNA.

I am not a coward, not timid, but I could only fear and cower from the harsh and ugly attacks.

Instead I find praying, always silently praying for kindness and for the strength to survive the attacks.

My prayers must have been heard—some church attendees came to my aid. They heard and saw the assault on me and, good Christians that they were, they rushed to my defense. My drunken attackers withdrew, sauntering back like worms to the liquor store. Incidents like these caused me to always stay indoor to prevent further humiliation and attacks.

CHAPTER 16

Beach Beautiful And Deadly

It is 1994; I am almost 16 years old.

The sun was blazing--a great day for an outing on the beach. My father, stepmother and a few other relatives from father's side of the family embarked on a four hour trip to the beach--63 Beach, in the Cinderella county of Berbice.

Guyana is divided into three main counties: Essequibo, Demerara and Berbice. Guyana is known as 'the land with many waters' and has the largest single drop waterfall, The Kaieteur Falls, botanical gardens and a national zoo, near Georgetown.

The Kaieteur Falls are part of the Kaieteur National Park, once nominated a World Heritage Site. Guyana's wild forests are home to some of the most diversified animal and plants in the world.

On our long ride there I could feel the tension and psychological distance from my relatives.

I was an outcast.

They were a clique, sharing inside jokes while laughing at me. This added fuel to my father's ire, giving him further license to degrade me and to blame me for anything that he deemed shameful, annoying or uncomfortable. It was always my fault.

I never knew why but it was.

CHAPTER 17

Ocean Tears

I did not need my relatives to tell me that I didn't belong there.

The negative energy and the distanced feelings from them were major hints. It was obvious. I was the source of their the eternal embarrassment.

I knew what was coming. I was always quiet and shy but somehow even that drew negative attention and persecution toward me.

I slowly allowed myself to drift away from the group. I walked to a quiet spot on the sand and sat down to reflect. I had been a loner since birth so the cold shoulder treatment situation was nothing new. I needed to relax. I found a moment of sorely needed bliss, still longing for my mother to return, for a miraculous change in my life...how long and when?

The sun was warm and the wind was soft and cool on my skin. I could have sat there forever and been content. This seemed to be better than any other place for my wounded soul. I could release things that I could not let go of before.

I knew my healing was not permanent or complete, but I hoped for some shift from past damaging thoughts.

I watched the waves rush in and clash against the rocks, slowly rolling over themselves again to regroup and start all over again. The feeling was euphoric, but I knew it was all about to change. Any hint of hope or happiness in my life was always short lived, disrupted by pain, sadness and disappointment.

I felt it, cold hard liquor drenching my head as cigarette butts and sea shells pelted me like hail. My ears rattled, recoiling from the vile expletives hurled my way. First I was dragged then hurled into the air like some dirty, deflated beach ball.

I had given up on life yet I was still walking, breathing, even talking upon the Earth. I was stuck, caught between places that meant unpleasantness and harm.

Fear blinds me. This is what happens when my mind and brain shut down. Thoughts and prayers became useless ghosts, delusions, as I felt the hands of several men and women on my body, dragging me towards the ocean and into the deep water. They were trying to drown me.

I sensed the approach of death so I fought, fought to survive. With all my remaining strength I struggled against their bodies, pushing myself up, away from their grasp.

I desperately needed air. I had to breathe. I felt strong hands around my neck, strangling me, force me back down. I knew this nightmare: I had to fight one more hard fight to awaken from horror.

Arms flailing, with my last ounce of strength, I made contact with someone, a woman, and I held on for dear life.

I was saved.

The men and two women released me from their grip and walked away.

I was still clinging to the woman who had saved me. She thought the whole thing was a joke. She thought we were all friends playing a silly game--water sports--so she did not intervene. Not until I held unto her arm without letting go.

Hurriedly I made my way back to where my father sat, doing my best to appear sane. I didn't want anyone to know about the attack. No one would believe, or worse still, they would actually blame me for provoking it. I could imagine my father apologizing to my assailants for the disturbance I had caused.

"You actually went into the water?" my cousin asked. I solemnly nodded.

About five minutes later the woman who saved me came and told my father and relatives about the attack. By that time my attackers were out of sight, nowhere to be found.

My dad actually thanked the woman for saving me (!), then told me to stay close by. I felt protected by my daddy for the first time but my pain, my near brush with death by drowning, overcame any other feelings.

I started to think, *Maybe Daddy does care about me.* He loved me in his own peculiar way.

CHAPTER 18

Flood Of Undying Memories

Saturday in Queens. I have eleven appointments.

Five are for haircuts, four for color and two new clients need extra special styling for a wedding and an engagement. They also want their makeup done.

Well, I still have time for coffee and a long hot shower.

But an admirer, Bryan, keeps crossing my mind. I am not sure: should I go out with him tonight?

I *should* play hard to get but it has been a few weeks--feels like *forever*--since I've been out.

Suppose I do decide to meet up with him--what should I wear?

Oh well... I'll think about it while I'm at the shop.

"Hello! Hello, is anybody there?"

The voice of my aunt. My *two* aunts (Julie and Jenny). They are always together and always make the same boisterous entrance.

I was working on my last client's hair and was grateful for the break in our conversation. I gave as good as I got: I replied in the same unnecessarily loud manner. We usually spoke in our colloquial Guyanese way.

It was about 7 p.m. My phone buzzed: a text from Bryan confirming our date.

"Pick me up around nine, okay?" I texted back.

The plan was dinner and drinks at a Thai restaurant. Thai food is one of my favorite cuisines, especially the pineapple fried rice.

The excitement of going out to dinner must have been written all over my face. Before I could finished my text my two aunts were all over me wanting to know everything: who it was, where I was going, what would I wear? They were disappointed that I was not going to join them at the local Indian restaurant. The place had good food and music, and they never tired of laughing at the drunken patrons.

They were concerned: they always warned me to be careful. I said I would be fine.

"Call us when you get home," they said.

No problem. I nodded

CHAPTER 19

Dressing For The Kill

As I look back on my many past relationships I now see my missteps, mistakes, wrong choices...but for some reason I am unable to correct them. I just seem to make them over and over again, always hoping for a different result.

But I don't know why. Why do I keep doing that?

As I pulled up the zipper of my sexiest dress, purchased from *a haute couture* designer's collection, I had flashbacks of other times, of other such preparations for dates that ended in disappointment.

I'm remembering an older, a much older man. His name is Doug and I now consider him irrelevant.

We met on a dating website. Doug is very rich, well-connected, and lives in Pennsylvania State. He was originally from Italy, which was exotic, really great.

The sex was abundant--no other way to put it. I was hoping to live in a big, beautiful house all worry no more about my victimhood behind me. I would be safe, free from the prison of my past.

Doug promised all this to me, promised me the best life I could imagine. We spent nights together and he took me to high end restaurants and other memorable places; money was no object. Some weekends he would come and stay almost the entire week. Then he would leave. He said he had important meetings to attend.

I loved him dearly.

But sometimes he would snap at me. Doug hid things from me. The relationship lasted nearly three years. I gave it my all and put up with much. Gradually--then finally--he was not there for me. Romeo Doug turned into abusive Doug. He began putting me down with insults, with condemnations that over time became increasingly frequent. None of my needs were being met yet I tolerated all of his verbal denigration.

All of my relationships had the same thing in common: abuse. I wasted almost three years on Doug. He kept on appearing and disappearing, back and forth in my life...until I found out that he was still happily married.

The buzz on my phone brought me back to reality. My date Bryan was waiting outside. I was a bit nervous as I peeked through the windows from my bedroom and watched him standing outside his car.

Wow! Nice car, I said to myself.

And how about that pink shirt?...hhhhmmm. It takes a real man to wear pink, I thought.

He looked great and smelled great, too.

"Nice dress," he said.

"Oh, thank you," I replied.

Dinner was not disappointing. I discovered that we had a friend in common--Pamela, whom he had dated. Not only that, but he was still in a relationship with her. And I was still friends with her.

We were unscrupulous.

That night Bryan and I ended up at his place, but not before we made one final stop.

He introduced me to the hookah after he offered me a drink. Afterwards we went back to his apartment: he had forgotten his driver's license, which he would need to drive me home. I knew it was a lie but I went along with it anyway. Bryan was definitely not boring and he kept me rapt in intelligent conversation.

I always admire a wise smart man.

I liked the hookah. It felt good; it tasted good too. Watermelon flavor, he told me. I was completely relaxed and remember almost every moment of that night. I couldn't reject his advances, even if I wanted to.

This was a man had been begging to take me out three years ago. Now I welcomed my chance.

We had sex in every possible position, more times than I could count. The passionate kisses, the caresses, the warm gentle touches and tender bites of an expert lover. All over my body. I love to be in control so I rode on top, blindfolding him with my underwear and handcuffing him with my bra. While wearing my red five inches stilettos heels.

It only made him beg for more--even after I dripped the hot melted candle wax all over his stomach. And worked our way in the steaming shower with honey followed by the barely touches of ice cubes dripping downwards while licking every melted drop.

He loved it.

And here I thought I was *soooo* shy. After all I'm a Scorpio, born in the month of November.

That night, after the exhausting work out at his place, he brought me home and we continued the steamy love session for hours until we were both totally spent from exhaustion. It was very late in the morning when he left.

Lying naked in bed after Bryan left I began reviewing all my past and present encounters. This was not unusual for me; these trysts and liaisons formed my life.

But as I lay there I felt strange--just like the night before. Minutes after smoking the hookah with Bryan my body felt out of control.

Why I was unable to stop what was happening to me? Why did I lose control of my body?

My God! He had drugged me.

I was sure. At the dinner table he asked if I ever smoked weed. I remember telling him I said no to drugs.

When I confronted Bryan about it he just laughed, then asked if I would like to smoke some weed.

That was the end of that relationship.

Even though every other experience with him was consensual I still could not fathom why he did what he did. I had started to like him, too...

I lay back down on my pillow and let my mind drift...way back to 1996, back to the old country--Guyana.

CHAPTER 20

Recollections

It has been over six years, when I was 18 years old, since my mother left Guyana for Venezuela to pursue a better life. A better life for *us*. We had no idea where she was and could not understand why she had not reached out to us all those years.

There were talks of her death, talk which seriously disturbed me. I had many sleepless nights worrying about her.

Every day survival, having to go out to the street to attend to errands or to work, only made the insomnia worse. My harassers were merciless with me, and my fear of men was wreaking havoc on my nerves.

1996 was a mixed year for me.

Easter and kite flying meant sadness. I had already (once again) left my father's house and had moved in with my next-door neighbor.

Who would want to move from their own parents at such an early age? The neighbors were kind. I had spent so much time in their home, cooking and cleaning for them, that they asked me to move in.

They knew of the severe abuse I had suffered at the hands of my father and step mother. I guess they felt sorry for me. The fact that I was an excellent cook (and still am!), didn't hurt. They accepted me into their home.

Blessed relief from the stress at home! I enjoyed the time we shared despite the short supply of down time. Shakeela, her sister Fazeela and I were all about the same age. We got along well.

I was released from my father's imprisonment.

Staying there, in the neighbors' house, was no bed of roses. There were insults and verbal abuse, mostly from the younger brother. However, they did their best to keep him from hurting me. Unlike his sisters, he was a tyrant.

The two sisters and I went to the park to celebrate Easter by flying a kite.

That did not end well.

I was attacked by several men whose kite had gotten tangled up in ours. They cursed at me and pushed me to the ground. One of them tried to rip my ear off with something that felt very sharp.

I was bleeding profusely as we were chased out of the park. I was the main target--not my friends, but me. I seemed to bring darkness on a shiny day.

Should I have locked myself away and let life pass me by?

A dark could hovered over me from the minute I was born. Happiness was not for me.

Was I cursed?

Maybe that's what it was: I was *cursed.* How else to explain the continuous unraveling of my life, make sense of the experiences thrust upon me? I had no parents and if anyone was going to love me, it had to be me.

It didn't matter whose house I was in. No matter whose house I was in I was still imprisoned, caged, marked with a scarlet letter for all the world to see. Despite my best intentions (I always tried to fit in), but somehow or other I always drew further attacks and violence toward me.

CHAPTER 21

Circle Of Life

Christmas and birthdays for my brother and I were celebrated--through the eyes of other children.

We did not see what most saw. We did not wake up to beautifully wrapped gifts under a tree. Year round we lacked for clothes and toys. We did not go to big places or restaurants. These things were just not part of our lives.

As you can see, we were poor. The poor do not have much. The rural area we lived in the middle of nowhere, a hole in the wall.

Those sweet things that most children received were missing from our lives. Our parents had to make do with the little they had; the children got the punches and blows that often came with impoverished, broken homes. Despite this, we were content; we dreamed that one day we too would enjoy such bountiful love.

Most children in American are brought up on Santa Claus: the big, fancy Christmas tree and some jolly bearded man coming down a hole he can barely fit through. It was different for us. Our clothing was tattered, our feet were bare, filthy from from the dirt and food scraps that were scattered about.

Today, I am filled with shame as I recall the many times my brother and I had to steal small amounts of cash from relatives and friends. We had no choice. It was either that or starve.

Money brought happiness to our bellies. Being hungry is a sin, we say--but so is stealing. I still pray to God to forgive my transgressions.

Being young and essentially parentless added to our naivete and misguided behavior. Many memories pop up, obscuring the better things I have going on in my life right now. I literally have to force--and pray--my way through them.

CHAPTER 22

Finally! One Good Christmas

It was December 23, 1996, one month after my 18th birthday. Birthdays were just another regular day for me; I never was able to have a birthday party.)

In walked my mother.

A mother is incomparable to anyone else on the planet. They give us life and the Great Mother receives us during death.

A mother can be defined as a nurturer, protector and a provider to say the least. The greatest source of love, comfort, and identity.

Euphoric? I was way beyond euphoric. My heart raced, stood still, then raced some more. The palms of my hands were hot and sweaty.

I remembered how to smile--yes, SMILE, with uncontrollable tears of joy.

To see my mother's face, to feel her arms around me to know she was still alive. Nothing mattered more.

The one who had given breath to me was stood there before me.

Thank you God. The joy of that moment replaced all the bad memories that came before.

My mom was accompanied by a man and a child. She had started her own family; she looked well and healthy--nothing mattered more.

Her years of fighting dad, surviving dad, is what kept her strong.

She said she had been hospitalized for months, following a fire in the pizza restaurant at which she worked in Venezuela. She had sustained burns over 50% of her body. There was more. She had undergone surgery to remove a brain tumor. a

She had been unable to contact us, she said. I couldn't process it all...but all that mattered was that *she was home.*

How come her new man had not tried to contact us, not tried to let us know what was going on? And now she had a child, my stepbrother... Questions and doubts raced through my mind. With all that recovery time why hadn't she contacted us, her nearly parentless children?

I had no answers. All I knew was that a mother's love was priceless. That is all I could focus on. I felt my stress melt away in seconds. Although my fears and uncertainty remained, being close to my mother made life worth living again.

The man in my mother's life stayed several weeks before returning to Venezuela. He too was Guyanese. He was a dentist who lived and worked in Venezuela.

He was married and had his own set of children.

My mom suffered a lot, endured great hardship from this man. I suspected as much, even before she shared anything about this with us. But we had our mother back. She met him after she was burned and lost everything. He took advantage of her highly dependent state and literally locked her indoor to prevent her from ever contacting the outside world.

There was another child, a sister.

After arriving in Venezuela my mother gave birth to my little sister. I had no idea that she was pregnant when she left. Her story--a pregnant mother leaving her home to work as a housekeeper in a foreign country--grew deeper and darker.

Immediately after she gave birth, my grandmother flew to Venezuela and returned with the child (my sister), who was then placed with one of my mother's sisters in Guyana. We had minimal contact with my aunt, who claimed that the little girl was her own--another whole complicated situation.

Soon after my mother arrived in Guyana I rented a house for the four of us (myself, my brothers and my mother).

Times were harder than ever for me I took care of all the bills but I did not mind. All I wanted was to be with my little family. Being alone had gotten old and the presence of the others gave me a feeling of comfort and safety. All I ever dreamed of was my family.

My new stepbrother was a year old and a bit spoiled, but he was so cute, so adorable, that we all loved him. I babysat when mother had to attend some family gathering, go to market, or had other errands to do.

I enjoyed these moments; lovely moments to be inscribed in my book of thoughts.

To this day I can't fully explain the way I treated my baby brother.

The events of my childhood must have brought out my rougher side. There were times, times that I became angry, when my tougher side emerged and showed through.

There was no reason to beat my one year old brother. I just did. I would beat him when he smiled, when he cried or if he got too close to me.

I would just beat him, mercilessly.

After beating him I would take him in my arms and hug him tightly, crying and saying how sorry I was. My outbursts were unpredictable, irrational, erratic. That is what you are thinking, and no doubt you are right.

Judge me if you will; Lord knows I am not beyond reproach. I feel deep sorrow every time I think of how I treated him. I still don't understand. Beatings were a regular feature of my childhood. Maybe I thought it was the right way to act; I didn't yet know how to love.

Maybe, maybe not. I needed therapy. Possibly a psychiatrist could help more.

Revealing all this is quite embarrassing--but this is my story. No one is perfect, least of all me.

I like dreaming. Dreaming gives me hope and brings me closer to what could be.

CHAPTER 23

Unrequited Love

I woke with a terrible headache, compounded by the fact that I had an appointment with my therapist in a couple of hours.

I took my college finals yesterday. I am beyond relieved. I never imagined that going into the medical field as a surgical assistant would be so difficult.

I had lots of help but memorizing all that medical and surgical information was no small matter: I might as well have become a full-fledged surgeon intstead of assisting one.

I feel a sense of pride, of accomplishment, considering where I have been and what I have experienced. Working in an operating room where I get to assist with surgeries is my single greatest achievement.

Succeed at this would mean less time in the hair salon. Not a problem: I already had a booth rented out. I needed two more people to rent out the rest.

Sleep is taking me over...

I see him now, as if it was yesterday. Handsome, chiseled, with a strong jaw, thick hair and a very smooth complexion. His name was Ravish.

Ravish was my first love, a love that came from the depths of my heart. A love that was neither forced nor demanded of me.

Ravish worked in the National Insurance accounting department in Guyana. He lived 20 minutes away from me and I met him was by chance.

We bumped into each other at the movie theatre in Georgetown. On my day off I went see a movie. Just to spend some time alone, or so I thought!

We slammed into each other as I was walked from the restroom. He was headed in the same direction. He followed me and took the seat right next to mine.

I remember the name of the movie: *Night Eyes 3*. It was an erotic film. One thing led to another and Ravish and I started flirting. He told me I was beautiful, that he was very attracted to me. I found myself nervous, shaking, and sweating.

From the very first we had an unspoken agreement: we would keep our relationship a secret. Still, I wanted to tell the whole world! But this was my first love relationship ever, and I was not about to spoil it by spreading the news. Besides, whom would I tell? I had no confidantes.

Our secret rendezvous took place three times a week in his small room. We had to be careful. I could not get enough of him, and he felt the same way about me, but our love and our love making was forbidden.Whenever I missed him, (which was all the time) I would call him at work, and he loved it. It kept us both stimulated and excited.

One month of this and then it abruptly ended.

Ravish avoided me at every turn. My phone calls went mostly unanswered. When it was answered, it was someone else he had asked to take the call. He wanted to get rid of me.

I spent many sleepless nights thinking about Ravish. Finally, I called his work, demanding to speak with him.

That was when my heart was shattered.

The girl who answered the phone took great pleasure telling me how disgusted Ravish was of me, how he never wanted to see me again. *I was not his type.* In the end she warned me of the beating he intended for me if I kept pursuing him.

The break up with Ravish fit perfectly in the same box I kept the rest of the torture, rapes, beatings and degradations I had endured. It was 1:30 when I awoke from this disturbing dream of my past love. Once again I had missed my appointment with Dr. Irene, but I needed sleep.

CHAPTER 24

Sunrise And Sunset

The passing of my father left me drained of any emotion.

February, 2001: the date of my father's death. He was hospitalized for about a month, diagnosed with kidney failure.

Years of alcohol abuse contributed to his kidney disease. I was worried about my father. I wanted him to live to a ripe old age; perhaps we would have been able to talk about his mistreatment of me. I felt guilty, too. I could not take care of him as most other children do with their older folks.

But he left us that day, far sooner than I expected. The next day we made the funeral arrangements. I took care of every expense. I felt like I did my share. Despite all the hurt, abuse and neglect my father doled out, I could never have ill will towards him. I know he loved me.

I took some solace in the fact that he found a small measure of peace in his final days. I wish I could have shared in that peace.

Living in our impoverished third world country--having only the most minimal education--contributed to his ignorance. But he loved me and I loved him back. Those are the facts. I ask God each day to allow me a forgiving heart and unending love for all, including my enemies.

I pray for his soul, and ask God to grant him forgiveness. Even now, as I write this, I wish he was alive. I wish he could have come to America and experience freedom.

He was born and raised in an ignorant society, and practiced ignorance until the day he died. If he were alive today he would have been able to travel out of that ignorant society and experience modern life with all the love the world has to offer. Maybe he would have enjoyed having his children at his side; unfortunately, he did not live to see that day. I still remember when I was very little, my daddy used to buy me ice cream whenever he had extra money, there are days that I still cry. I cried sometimes when I wish he was here as we gotten closer before he passed away. I understand why he was ignorant and violent towards me. He thought by doing what he did was going the change me to his expectations but that still wasn't the way to act towards a child.

CHAPTER 25

Walking Through The Valley Of The Shadow Of Death

At age 23 years I was managing a video shop. The work was not especially hard.

I loved what I did but people, things, and sometimes the place itself work against one's peace of mind and ability to succeed.

Running a business is not all fun and games! You have to invest much time and effort into creating a successful workplace. There were good days and there were bad days. Some nights were overwhelming.

Running your own business takes determination. and though an income is not guaranteed, the way it is in a 9 to 5 job, the freedom of being your own boss is well worth the wait.

I had taken off a week for my father's funeral; this was my first day back. For some reason I just don't feel like being here. Uneasy and restless, I kept looking towards at the clock, hoping that closing time would come. Closing time is nine each night and, as usual, as that time approached I always got tense and nervous, considering the neighborhood my store was located in.

Georgetown: so different from New York City, yet its shadow seemed to follow me wherever I went.

No matter that New York was affluent. Thoughts of being attacked or of being 'found out' still troubled me.

Probably just my mind was playing tricks on me.

I was no longer trapped in violent hostile Guyana. Being here in New York was awesome. America was the land of opportunity, and the food basket of the world.

This perspective helped me maintain a good steady mindset: crazy New York streets were far better than the streets at home.

At the stroke of nine that night I locked the door and proceeded to count the cash in the register. Usually this takes 20 to 30 minutes.

Locking the doors of the store behind me, I hurried down the street towards the bus stop. It is was about a five minute walk but the entire area seemed particularly dark and dangerous that night.

Five yards from the bus stop I approached two big, shadowy trees on the right side of the street. There I was bum rushed by at least six men, who knocked me down and dragged me from the road to the dark edge of the sidewalk under the tree.

Just like old times. Tragedy followed tragedy, as though I was put upon this earth to receive hurt and pain. My head was spinning, my mind was racing and my throat was dry. Unbearable misery and speechlessness visiting me again.

The assailants' angry words were very confusing. They were accusing me of voting for and taking part in the opposition party's propaganda in the recent election.

All of this was untrue, absolutely senseless. Just a flimsy excuse to attack me.

Suddenly I saw the shiny blade of a knife; the next moment, its cold, hard metal pressed hard at the bottom of my eye.

"I am going to dig out your eyes with this knife," said the man. "And then we're going to take turns raping you...and ripping your apart."

One of the others chimed in, "We will cut you open and do whatever we want with you."

Did they think about what they were doing? Would they attack their mothers this way? Or were they cold, conscienceless, not caring about--or even enjoying--terrorizing others?

My belief in the goodness and kindness of others was unreal, a treasured illusion that dissolved away...

I heard my screams in my head, but they could not come out of my mouth. I felt pieces of me being torn like it was nothing.

I was nothing.

Scary untangled threads of similar moments in my life flashed through my mind. Nothing but shame and guilt had entered my heart from the second this all started.

Who would save me?

I kept hope alive, maybe I could be saved. I felt the bile in my stomach float to my throat, threatening to suffocate me, and still I was unable to scream. Fear has paralyzed my throat along with my entire body.

Suddenly, I felt pain: my hair being chopped from my head with a knife by a different assailant. Next my pants were viciously ripped from my lower body.

I always wear leggings under my jeans (a precaution born of the countless times I had been attacked and molested and viciously raped.) My only defense was to wear as many undergarments as possible.

That was the only way I knew to fight back.

Then I felt a sharp pain in my shoulder as my undergarments were cut away.

The sound of a vehicle, the focused glare of bright lights on us, saved my life. I felt the many hands of my attackers release me, and as they ran from fear of being caught I could hear them shouting at me, "If you tell the police we will hunt you down and kill you in 24 hours." They yelled the very same words as the others who had harmed me in my life.

I wish that the strength I have now I had back then. The driver of the car took me to the Georgetown Public Hospital where I was treated with stitches on my elbow and on two other parts on my body.

I then lied to my mother when I got home. I told her that I had a fall at work while trying to stock the shelves with video cassettes and DVDs. Regardless of how one judged her, my mother always worried about us--mothers always know their children best. I was not what they expected--why? Just because I loved differently. My body said one thing and my heart said another.

CHAPTER 26

More Pain, Yet Hope Is Reborn

Tonight I am going to watch another new premier Lifetime movie.

The movie is about the triumph of good over evil and victory over temptations: the defeat of adversaries.

I put on the television and flipped through the channels. I saw "Breaking News. Man burns woman to death."

This also impacted me. I thought about *my* past experiences with burns and men. Throughout my life, despite its ups and deep deep down, I continued grasping at hope, recalling that the sun that rose every day, vanquishing the night.

I could not allow any more rain to drown my parade. Life had already thrown too many sticks and stones my way. I was excited about the up and coming holiday.

Our traditional and festive National Republic Day dispelled my gloom.

Many in our country took this day seriously. The celebration gave renewed hope to the community. The holiday was comparable to the The Fourth of July in the U.S.A.

When it comes to holidays we go above and beyond. The festivities and spectacle make for one of the brightest points of the year.

This is the anniversary of the date when Guyana became a republic and it signifies freedom from slavery. You will see crazy outbursts, people who look like they have been in hiding, waiting for this day to arrive.

Guyana celebrates *Mashramani* every year on February 23. The day marked our continuing fight for freedom from slavery begun in 1763. This is well known as the Slavery Rebellion.

The fight against slavery continued, with another revolt in 1823, the Demerara Rebellion. As many as 13,000 slaves rose up against their oppressors. The rebels were crushed but their righteous cause continued. By 1838 total emancipation was achieved.

Our ancestors rebelled, fight to protect their region and their rights and they won. This movement caused many Europeans to flee; only half of them remained.

Despite the abolition of slavery, Guyana remained under British rule until the 20th century. Then, in 1966, it became an independent country. During the time of celebration all of the country gathers and rejoices with dancing, with music, and with performing artists. Parades pass through the street, featuring large floats that takes days and weeks to construct. All types of people are on the streets, waving Guyana flags and dressed in ethnic attire. Imagine thousands of humans gathered for one big party, a one day carnival.

You can barely see over your shoulder; the only way to be heard is by yelling. The parade is a beautiful sight, a living commemoration and memorial to what our brave ancestors endured.

My co-worker Bibi invited me out to the grounds to enjoy the day. This was much needed down time so I agreed to go. What harm could it do?

She reassured me that she would watch over me like a hawk. I had no intention of getting very involved; I just wanted to step back and watch from the sidelines. I trusted Bibi. Our relationship had grown tighter.

Ever since we started working together I assumed that I could accept her in my life. Life is all about change, constant change, so I had to eventually deal with not seeing her that much.

I was happy when Bibi and I worked the same shift. She had a laugh that could wake an entire neighborhood, that might even break glass. It was good having her around to support me, to be there for me.

I longed for that kind of friendship and our time together at the parade. I was able to relax for a while. We enjoyed ourselves, enjoyed all the extravagant and beautiful moments as day became night.

We decided to leave before it got too late. It was getting dark. The parade goers were still walking round the streets filled with cheer. Pushing our way through a thick mass of shoulders and dancing revelers we encountered a group of guys.

I had not particularly noticed them--but they had noticed us. They reminded me of a pack of lions waiting to devour a piece of raw meat in the wild. They were sitting outside a bar near the parade route, barbecuing their chicken on a grill.

I remember the scene like it happened yesterday.

The bar was on Vissengen Road in Georgetown, right along the way to Bibi's car. It was like some Discovery Channel travelogue, showing the lions sniffing the air as they got closer and closer, ready to attack.

They hollered at us from across the street and trying their vociferous best to get our attention. We were trying to reach home, chalking it off as a good day.

As they came into view my friend Bibi began to cry for help. Things quickly escalated. Maybe these guys had seen me before, perhaps at the video club I recently worked.

Things just got worse. These guys were not just after Bibi but they were going for me as well. I screamed out as they attacked me, hearing their horrible voices, their descriptions of how they would hurt me. Crazy: the day had gone so well, only to turn into another nightmare.

I had felt an aching pain in my heart from the combined humiliation and embarrassment. Dealing with this--not to mention the crowds of people that stood around--was degrading, in the extreme. I mean, getting trapped in such a situation while everyone else milled at a safe distance. Another shameful moment.

"I'm not who you think I am! I'm not what you think I am!" I screamed out, trying to get them to back off. Screaming out didn't help one bit.

You would think the others around would intervene, would somehow try to stop the situation...but no one came to save us. I was speechless now, profoundly ashamed, being dragged across the street like that in full view of the others.

They pulled me closer to their grill, dragging me towards the fire. Brutally, I was forced closer to the hot coals until my shoulders and stomach were burned. One of the assailants wielded a stick of burning wood. Bibi reached for me, barely saving me in time.

She caught me before they could burn my face. Running, we reached Bibi's place and caught our breath, now that we were safe. I hid everything that happened from my mother, not wanting to burden her any further with my pain: business as usual.

The streets of my country had become as much of a prison as my father's house had been. No matter where I went the abuse followed me, like a shadow, like a faithful dog...this time it was done by strangers and not by someone I knew.

Before we reached my house Bibi took me to the police station. She insisted. As we went she suggested that all this had to stop, that I should change my voice, my clothes, my lifestyle, and not be the person I really was.

Become a normal person--stop inviting this misery upon myself--and all these trouble would end.

Little did she know, but I always tried. I tried so hard to fit in, to conform, but somehow I seemed to be inviting more tragic moments into my life. The moments of encountering humiliation and threats were innumerable. I endured the same kind of attacks at the video store.

At times I had been abused and accused by Guyanese attackers--no surprise!--who threatened to kill me. The justified their violence by assuming that I had voted for the Indian President.

Guyana has a history of false political allegations, many of these quite crazy. I was ridiculed at work simply because of my appearance. Even though PNC (the opposition party) was right upstairs from where I worked I didn't get many threats from them...they just stared as they stood at the entrance.

One incident followed another, but the parade was a welcome break from these, while it lasted. In this world, we must choose wisely so that we do not add to the pain that the world always seems to offer.

CHAPTER 27

Farewell

I said my goodbyes and left Guyana in late 2002, hoping to find work in Brazil.

I planned for all to go well and hoped to be able to work my way to the top. I could not get a job the week I was there and had to figure out what I would do next. It was dreadful: I had to accept the fact that I could not find work and once again pack my bags for Guyana.

Flying on an airplane for the first time was exciting, a truly great experience. I felt like I was flying away from everything and everyone, away from pain. But I was wrong.

Totally wrong.

Days went by and I found myself in an internet café chat room, which kindled a flame inside me. Here I met, via the internet, a guy named Prince.

It sounds unrealistic, to think you and another person online could actually build a future together, huh? Growing up I knew nothing about the internet or any related technology. This stuff was all new to me but I always enjoyed learning and expanding my horizon. (Eventually education rescued my life.) I took a crash course in computer 101. I wanted to pursue education so that I would not have to depend on anyone for anything.

Survival was my priority.

Today, in the U.S., I am still learning. Sometimes I feel like a newborn in an adult body.

We had our long conversations and I found myself, once again, packing to leave. We would meet in the Bahamas to meet him sometime in April, 2003.

My life had always been chaotic. So I thought, *how bad could this be?*

I asked my aunt Pam and she sent me a plane ticket to the Bahamas. (Pam lives here in the U.S. and it was her home that I went to and stayed at after release from of the detention center.)

She and I grew close over time and, despite being my youngest aunt, Pam was became my surrogate mother figure. I got all the financial and other support from her. (She cut my hair off the next day after I moved in!)

She too thought I could change.

Anyone searching for a replacement of love that they never got can surely relate.

My stay in the Bahamas lasted about two months.

I had graduated in Guyana as a nail technician so there were a lot of jobs and people wanting to hire me but in order to get a job in the

Bahamas I had to leave the island, apply for a work permit, then return to the Bahamas.

But I could not have afforded it financially and the sexual harassment three times a night from Prince was unbearable. Besides, there was no one else to turn to. Prince worked at a local gas station in the Bahamas and tried to help me but he was struggling himself.

Once again the emotional roller coaster was rising and falling.

The last day of my stay there I was forced to buy my return ticket to Guyana. I had tried and failed; nothing else seemed possible anymore.

At least I knew what to expect back at home--death.

I could not go back there, to that jail. It seemed as if the entire country was against me; the land that I grew up in and called home was toxic to my very being. I knew little else but this prison. Was I destined to be chained there forever?

CHAPTER 28

Land Of Liberty

After I bought my air fare and walked out of the travel agent's office I sat in a park not far away. It was a beautiful Saturday afternoon, July 5th, 2003.

In the midst of my daydreaming I was brought back to reality when an older black woman approached me saying, "My child, why are you crying? You are so young and beautiful, who and what can possibly be the reason for your hurt? Girl, you better wipe those tears." She was short, about 4 feet 4 inches tall, with gray hair, brown skin, and she was a pearl white dress. Her English was fluent and she descended upon me like a merciful angel.

I was still searching for peace. I told her my story. She shocked me. She said regardless of what I had been through I was still beautiful, and that God is testing my faith. Prayers, music and Lifetime movies were, and still are, my therapy.

Prayers gave me faith, yes, lots of faith. Faith in the belief that there is always a better tomorrow.

Music eased my distress and practically every Lifetime movie made me aware like I was not alone, that I was not the only one suffering. The music and the movies gave me hope for a better life ahead. Those were the strengths I lived by. The words of that old lady still echo in my ears to this day.

"I am sorry you have been through all those horrible things but your life is not over yet," she continued. "You are on this Earth for a big, big reason and I assure you that you will see it one day. Now, since your flight is stopping in Miami and you have to change planes why don't you ask for political asylum?"

I never heard of any words like 'political asylum' before but all else had failed. Would asking for asylum change anything or make a difference?

The flight was short, 40 minutes in all from the Bahamas. I landed at Miami International Airport the evening of July 5th around 5 p.m. I did not have a visitor's visa so I could not leave the airport. In fact, when the plane landed I was detained by an immigration officer who walked with me to a room. I was supposed to stay locked in that room for the next two hours until my flight back to Guyana was ready to board. I had just landed here in the U.S.A., the melting pot of the world yet I was not allowed to explore or see this wonderful land.

After about an hour in custody I told the officer that I did not want to go back to Guyana because I feared for my life, that I would like to apply for political asylum.

She looked at me like '*What?*'

"Excuse me, what did you just say?"

I told her again that my life was in danger. She called another officer, who came and tried to convince me to go back home and that if I lost in the asylum process that I would be banned from the United States for a period of ten years or more. I would not be able to visit or see my grandparents ever.

I had been refused a visitor's visa twice before but now that I was already here I was willing to take that chance.

"I don't care if that happens, sir, but I want to apply for asylum," I told him.

I was treated like a criminal throughout the whole process. But there was no way I was going back. I knew there was light on the other side--on these shores--so I chose asylum.

I may have been put in an actual prison but I was closer to freedom than ever before. With all the struggles and abuse I received growing up, and with all that abuse still waiting for me at home, I knew this was the only way I might have a life. A life that was free.

Later that night I was interviewed by another officer, who ruled on my stay in a detention center. He said I would get my chance to speak to an asylum officer. If that officer determines that you have a credible fear of returning to your country you will then have the opportunity to speak with an immigration judge. That judge will then decide if you get to stay in the U.S.A.

The next morning I was transferred to a detention center in Miami,

Florida. Three days later I was sent to the Elizabeth Detention Center in New Jersey.

It was the most horrible flight ever. I was chained across my legs and the handcuffs bit at my wrists as I walked to and from and through the entire airports.

Can you imagine someone looking at you, thinking you are a criminal? That's is how I felt: numb, ashamed but going with the flow. I didn't have a choice.

I remained in detention for exactly two months and three days. This was by far one of the strangest experiences I had known. I was inside a dormitory with 40 other men.

These moments were awkward, uncomfortable in the extreme: I was the closest thing to a woman they had probably seen in years. All eyes to were on me from the very first day.

As attention arose I asked to be put in protective custody inside the prison for my own safety. That was not a pretty sight. The little prison was a cold place to be put into and a hard place to lay one's head at night. I still kept hope alive: it was safer for me inside than out. One small toilet and a twin sized bed with mattress made of papers instead of sponge, at least so it felt. Nothing was real and I was very confused and scared. I worried about my health and I wondered if I would ever get out. I thought I would go insane. Some detainees had been there over four years waiting for their case to be called or to be deported.

Writing my story--writing, writing, writing--kept me from losing my mind.

While in custody I watched a security guard stand out front to secure my door. One day in the month of September 2003 as I was in realm and was awoken by one of the guards around 4:30 a.m. He told me it was time for me to leave.

There was an explanation to the seeming miracle: my grandmother retained an attorney and finally I was let off on parole. The only condition was showing up for my court dates. So I actually spent two months and three days in detention center in New Jersey

Things were looking up!

I was was eternally grateful for being able to live with my grandmother in New York City. (This was the time that my aunt Pam snipped off my hair, hoping to change me back. I had no choice but to respect her will. After all, I was going to reside in her home.)

Now, many people hear the words *political asylum* but without wholly understanding what they mean.

In the United States asylum may be given to people who are afraid to return home because of persecution on account of their race, religion, nationality, social group or political persuasion. If you are granted asylum you can live and work in the U.S.A. and, after one year, you can file adjustment of status to become a permanent resident.

To start the process a person seeking asylum must be in a U.S. territory. To ask for asylum a 'USCIS' form must be filled out in its entirety; the processing is completed within 180 days of the date of filing.

This was definitely a step in the right direction. As I stayed with my grandmother at my aunt's house I started to look around and then was hired as a nail technician. I did what you would expect: file nails and provide a great deal of customer service.

One woman spoke to me about going to beauty school. Beauty school certification is well known in New York State. There is competition for jobs in the better salons but there still seemed to be room for me.

I took the woman's advice and encouragement, thanked her, and enrolled in a school. I learned many trades in beauty school; soon enough I was on my way to graduating as a cosmetologist and beautician. This was a life-changing event that would do me well.

After 18 months in beauty school I graduated, with beauty degree in hand. I hope the tale of my remarkable transformation motivates and inspires others who have all but given up.

No pain, no gain. You either keep hope alive or you give up.

My advice? I say, *Don't give up!* Trouble does not always last and that is a fact (in other words, 'This too shall pass.'). We sometimes do not get to pick and choose what comes our way but we can always try to keep our hearts and minds prepared for what may come. I had graduated and now was working inside a local salon.

This was freedom to me.

I slowly built up my clientele and eventually owned my own salon. The key to my freedom was now in *my* hands. I began to be happy with my life and all that it had brought me.

I managed my finances to the point where I could afford my own apartment. I moved out from under my aunt and grandmother: another stepping stone to independence.

CHAPTER 29

Transformation

I had this one question in my mind: when would I be able to afford my surgery? It was my most pressing desire.

A thumbnail sketch of the costs involved: before the actual surgery there was mandated at a cost of $50 to $200 per session.

Letters from two or more therapists are usually needed for surgery of this kind. They say the total cost of therapy and the letters can range from under $1,000 to more than $5,000 per year. Hormone therapy cost an additional $300 to $2,400 per year.

$40,000 for the operation itself.

This is what people contemplating this kind of surgery go through. Myself, I was just happy about being able to finally start living my life the way I wanted to, without external constraints (although I was still living in a West Indian community in Richmond Hill, Queens.)

The next step in my journey to transformation involved taking the necessary medication.

Things had definitely changed, of course, by the time my surgery took place. The strength and muscle power that got me through my chores in Guyana were gone after the surgery.

Part of me felt weaker but there was no change in my sense of who I was. The only change I could feel was physical.

After surgery I started to gain weight, picking up pounds as my body changed shape. Parts of my body, like the area around my hips, grew larger; I was a full-blown woman, curves and all, at this point. I was told that I had now become a woman, 100% female.

I think back on my fantasies, my daydreams as a child. They helped me get through the years of abuse, whether physical, sexual or verbal.

Now, when I look at myself, I see my daydreams alive in the real world. A world I always wanted to live in. I am now so encourage to live life and wants to explore and learn about different things and meet different people.

CHAPTER 30

Getting Better All The Time

With a referral from my attorney I reached out and began to piece the puzzles of my inner self together with psychological help. I wanted to face my fears and mend all of me: one whole person, one whole self.

There is danger in living without facing our demons. Knowing this helped me tremendously as I went from doctor to doctor for help. I received much love and felt grateful every step of the way.

I felt a little stronger each day. I didn't need to be institutionalized on a psychiatric ward. I was clearly strong enough to face the many challenges that I had and honest enough to reach out for the help that I needed.

Although I had much pain I chose to pick myself up and not allow the weight of the world to drag me down. Being an inspiration to others is one of my main motivation now. Giving advice and suggestions to clients in the salon only drew people closer to me. Everyone has a story to tell, just like the scars on my body. More and more people looked up to me for support and guidance.

Receiving my degree as a surgical technologist was the icing on the cake. As a surgical technologist you assist with the surgeries in the operating room. Maintaining sterility and anticipating a surgeon's needs in the operating room is essential; but being human, remaining in the moment and maintaining focus is very rewarding as well.

From the beginning I knew that I wanted to to do something more than run a beauty salon. Doing my research online I ran across the words *lab technician.*

So many conflicting thoughts ran through my mind. I asked myself, *"At this age could I honestly fulfill the qualifications and concentrate on my studies, especially science?"*

I also came across the words *surgical technologist.* Right away I knew this was it: this would be the place for me. I was highly fascinated by every aspect of the operating room after undergoing surgery myself. This was my dream: to assist a surgeon and assist in the life-and-death world of the operating room.

I got my degree and began to work in the field, a vey happy employee. It felt good knowing I had graduated with a college degree, motivating me even further to expand my education in the future.

Like most girls, I would like to get married and have lots of children one day. I hope to give my kids the love that I never had.

My life in Richmond Hill, in Queens, NY, is not bad at all. But like anywhere, it has its problems too. This place makes me think of home, of how provincial it was.

I have received much respect and admiration. Of course, I still have moments of discrimination from narrow-minded ones who notice the transition.

Such moments no longer bother me but the thought of what others may go through does. Many people need education, need to have their awareness level raised regarding abuse of all kinds. This society can no longer afford ignorance and intolerance. It is sinful--dead wrong--to bash and abuse those who are perceived as different.

I know of the murder of many men, women and children. I want this put to a stop. Regardless of what others may think, I consider myself a woman of dignity who is worthy of respect and praise.

My studies are a work in progress; I still hope to pursue other surgical areas.

"There is nothing like a mother's love," is the bottom line for me. The statement that is true and real and always holds its weight. My mother migrated to the United States six years ago.

She has been one of my major support systems along this journey of transition. I love and honor my mother--just as any newborn would.

Not only do I have her support but I now have the support of my grandparents and the rest of my family every step of the way. It amazes me how the relationships with my family have grown, how good it feels to have them by my side. My family now spends a lot of time with me. My cousins show me great respect and in fact look up to me an elder.

I give thanks to those friends that I gained and those who have given me loyalty and trust along the way. I did not depend on them as much as they would have allowed, but I am deeply thankful for their presence, which helped me overcome the obstacles in my way.

I started to expand my life, and had the privilege of meeting other artists and actors in the community. Organizations did open my mind to more possibilities and had my story featured in a play, *Tara's Crossing*.

The play was well received in schools; it highlights the immigration and detention situations around the U.S. *Tara's Crossing* has played in many colleges across the country to illustrate struggles like mine.

This was an inspiration to me and was produced to give inspiration to others, especially when I was present and offered advocacy and support in the after show talk backs that followed each performance.

I decided to share my life story with The Caribbean Equality Project. The Caribbean Equality Project focuses on advancing social change in everyday life, on making people more aware and on inspiring the community. This too has proven to be a good platform for advocating change.

I was also interviewed in one of the installments of the 'Self-Made Successful Women'. I got to answer questions about myself and my somewhat unique story. I got to describe how I had bettered my life.

The first question directed at me was "What is your definition of success?"

I replied, "My definition of success: success is about getting back on your feet after failure or getting up after a fall. As a survivor of torture, keeping a desire reach a goal is indeed a kind of success to me. My daily routine is always prayers. Being spiritual helped me a lot, especially with finding out more about who I am and what I was going through. I have been on a vegan diet for 14 years. My biggest challenge was being born different and I wanted to heal myself because my body said one thing while my mind said another. My advice to younger people who are going through what I went through is you are not alone, and *I know your pain*. I may not have experienced the same torture as you but believe me, I've been there. fNothing is permanent, not even pain. It can just be temporary, especially in today's fast-moving world. Your voice can be heard so let your voice be heard, please let your voice be heard. Because only you have that power to make a change and make a difference."

This quote is the mantra I live by. Wherever I go and whatever I do I always try to give it my best, so that my work will be praised and my style admired. I want to show that if one believes and has the hope of faith, people can make it through whatever they may be facing on their journey.

Keep fighting with determination in your heart and accept who you are. At the end of the day I believe we all have a strong desire for inner peace and should give ourselves such peace everyday!

The life I live now? I spend it watching *Lifetime* stories that influence my daily deeds. These shows inspire me to push ahead in my faith and everyday living.

Lifetime has its commercial side, but my focus is on the good that they do with their daily broadcast. My story is a prime example of there being a light at the end of the tunnel.

You cannot give up; you must remain strong-willed to make it out of your situation. You must love yourself first, then anything is possible.

Anything is possible.

Things in my life have gotten better and better. I have been approached and asked out on dates by men in high society, including doctors, lawyers and even police officers.

This next story is about one of my dates--the closest that came towards becoming another actual relationship.

I decided to go on a date with Doctor Lee.

Coming close to love was a beautiful thing for me. The doctor had another friend, Dr. Schwartz, who was a co-worker. Both are oral maxillofacial surgeons and I ended up going on three dates with Dr. Schwartz as well.

It might sound bad, or self-indulgent, but my dating life was quite wild. I admit it: I also enjoyed the wining and the dining at almost every expensive restaurant in New York City.

This was very exciting for me, navigating through life's sometimes funny, sometimes tangled situations. As it turned out, Doctor Schwartz was married, though; I certainly could not blame myself for that. As they say, "If you knew better, you would do better."

These episodes were transient, ephemeral. Lee was the guy that I had developed feelings for before all this occurred and my longing for him escalated quickly. He was one of those surgeons who got what he wanted, when he wanted it, and with whomever he wanted it with.

I was deeply attracted to him. He caught my eye before the friend ever did. Call me crazy, but I was still dating Dr. Schwartz, his friend. On a day to day basis Lee and I would work beside each other, mostly during surgeries. In this we grew closer and more attached to one another.

We made eye contact at every opportunity, luring one another in deeper and deeper. Feeling his gloves against mine as we worked surgical cases only upped the ante.

A connection was undoubtedly there. Sooner or later this would lead to something--some kind of commitment?--at least as far I was concerned. All this eye contact, the inadvertent touch of hands--these kind of events usually lead to a date. The question was, did he know?

Did he know about me and my change? What if he found out?

I had hidden it for all this time and this might cause him to turn to me and put a halt to what was happening between us.

I could not take more disappointment, could not endure another heartbreak. But still I took the chance and I will tell the next man I fall in love with about my true self.

First, though, I have to make sure he is someone who deserves my love and trust.

After many begging pleading phone calls from Dr. Lee I agreed to go on some casual dates with him: he was not all that appealing.

His breath smelled bad, he was possessive and he wanted to control me. He had psoriasis, which he did not take care of. He worked out a lot but that didn't validate his need to feel that he was is in charge of everyone and everything all the time.

His friend Dr. Schwartz tried to warn me about his controlling behavior but I guess I had to experience it for myself. I should not be fearing Lee's power over me just because of his elevated status in society. People in power---authority figures like a police officer, a doctor, even the president--should practice extra empathy and kindness, not provoke fear.

In fact, I greatly respect them, but what matters at the end of the day is being a human who serves humanity. Only then can one know inner peace and gain the respect of others.

I was still rejoicing at my change in fortune, going on dates with Dr. Schwartz or occasionally going locally with friends for happy hour or dinner exploring NYC.

That is when Dr. Patel, an anesthesiologist at the same hospital, saw me and said that he was crazy about me. He wanted to take me out. Very much wanted to take me out. We exchanged phone numbers and he kept on asking me out. I asked him for some time to think about it. He claimed that he had eyes for me for months and was attracted to me but had been too shy to approach me about his situation. He was considerably younger than me; he was hot. He was tall, dark and good-looking, an Indian hunk of a doctor.

After a day or two he started contacting me again but I wanted to keep it casual. My anxiety about disclosing my change still had the upper hand. Speaking of the name Patel...I have to go to the mall because I need powder and mascara for my date at the the movies tonight with (another) Dr. Patel. Yes, a second Dr. Patel who like Patel #1 was also an anesthesiologist.

Looks like I may end up with one Dr. Patel or another, but hey, you never know what life holds in store. We met during happy hour at a bar where he introduced himself to me. Walked right up to ask if I was a model because I looked and walked like one. He was mesmerized by my look and by my 5 inch heels.

I asked him if he had modeling connections and we became very close friends over time. (He was not the first man who proposed modeling.)

This doctor (Patel #2) and I became good friends. Very good friends. He was older and hoped for something intimate in the future but I kept it as just friends. He was going through a divorce (he claimed that his wife cheated on him repeatedly.) I was always there for him.

I am glad he trusts me as a friend, glad that he had someone--me--to lean on. I gave him advice and tried to make him feel positive about his future. He listened carefully to all my criticisms and suggestions. He had court the following day for the final decision on custody of his three children.

He was a doctor and a professional--yet he was scared, never having faced a judge before. My thoughts returned to December 1, 2003 when I appeared in immigration court for my final decision.

The judge was very tough, being an immigrant herself. I was especially scared because she was said to deport and deny peoples' applications to stay in the U.S. Maybe the rumor was wrong. Maybe she hated having to deport immigrants.

That morning, as I arrived at the court house with my attorney and my grandmother at my side, the judge started hearing cases. Soon enough it was my turn. I entered alone with my lawyer. As my lawyer submitted the supporting documents the judge called me up to the witness stand.

The judge was about 5 feet 7 inches tall. I turned to face the clock. My heart raced, considerably faster than the ticking of the clock. My fate was in the hands of this grey haired, brown skinned judge.

She leafed through the papers while thinking about her decision. I grew numb watching this judge quietly weighing my future.

Oh my God! What if she denied my application for political asylum? My heart beat harder and harder.

After looking through all the papers the judge asked me two questions. I felt like the dark brown walls of the courtroom would come crashing down on top of me. I started to shiver and perspire heavily, all at the same time.

"Defendant! Tell me, what did you think the reason was that you were persecuted and attacked in your home country? And how would you feel and what would you do if you are granted asylum, knowing that you will not be able to travel back to Guyana if something should happen to your mother or brothers?" she bellowed.

"Your Honor," I began. "My mother would be very happy to know that I am safe and that's very important to her. I was subjected to abuse, to rape, and I was beaten, stabbed, burnt and even stoned just because of who I am. You see, since I was five years old I have always felt like a girl even though I wasn't born as one. These feelings became stronger as I grew up even though I visited many doctors over the years. I went to Dr. Delamita and Dr. Sheere, who are both endocrinologists specializing in hormonal therapies. The doctors kept saying that I was born with more female hormones than male hormones and strongly recommended sexual reassignment surgery, a sex change."

Her fixed, stern glare offered little comfort but I did not despair. I couldn't read her thoughts. Her countenance betrayed little of what she was thinking or how she would rule.

"Being born in a third world country filled with ignorance and bigotry, it was hard and painful for me, and it invited persecution and torture upon my life," I continued. "So today, as a transgendered woman, I am seeking political asylum based on my gender identity and imputed sexual orientation."

After hearing this the judge made her final decision.

"In the matter of Veemala Persaud, a male who strongly looks like a girl and identifies as one. This application for asylum is…"

Conclusion

Today I am in a safer place. My life has been a roller coaster ride with its ups and downs and twists and turns. I survived terrible ordeals and a state of constant fear yet I was eventually able to spring back and enjoy things and to get on with my life.

The prisons of the past – my father's house, my aunt and uncle's domination, the men of my country – are behind me now and can no longer do me harm.

I am free. One taste of freedom and there was no going back. There are those who still try to denounce me, even now. They show up when I do motivational speeches or after I am on a video speaking out against abuse.

They verbally assault me, trying to put me back in that prison--but there is no going back. Many people condemn me by quoting the Holy Bible. The Holy Bible also mentions that if a man or a woman conceives out of wedlock they should be stoned to death. Jesus also said that whoever is born without sin should cast the first stone at a sinner. So what makes me an abomination before the Lord?

The learning experiences have made me tough--Army strong. Who was it who once said, "Whatever doesn't kill me outright makes me stronger?" I have fought a fight that many did not survive, but my survival and my story are gifts given to me to share with you.

I am still growing each day, trying to be the best person I can. I hope that reading this will help you because this is truly why we are here--to help each other, to unite.

My accomplishments reveal what is reachable to you. Never put a limit on what you can do. Simply show how much you can achieve--and then some! Far too often we let our external environment (or ourselves) put a limit to what we can do. We are always capable of more! I am a living witness to that. Endurance, patience and faith make almost anything being possible.

My family life has improved considerably. I now have much closer relationships with my aunts who live in America. My mother continues to be my source of inspiration. My brother will soon be a graduate from college.

The family members who are close to me now accept me and I welcome their love. It is the love I searched for as a child and have now found as an adult. And my mother, who I remember looking so small at the hands of my father's abuse, proved to me what *real* strength was. She lived through so much--abuse, sickness, poverty--yet persevered through it all. Because of that strength, she was able to come to America and see me graduate from school. Strength comes in all shapes and sizes.

There are my many lessons I cannot put on the blackboard of those going through trials similar to mine. I have reached out to many lives and hope for more opportunities to speak and inspire and motivate others.

Most who go through the vicious cycles of abuse and neglect do not speak out, but I encourage them to speak out--don't hide your stories! Fear breeds more fear; speaking out breeds courage, which leads to strength and more success.

My interviews with people throughout the city have further inspired me to speak my story out loud. I now have the courage to push forward. Protecting and saving the vulnerable, the innocent--children in situations similar to mine--are my source of inspiration. I advocate ZERO TOLERANCE for child abuse or neglect.

This message should be publicized, should be broadcast around the world.

Anything less is neglect or abuse.

Abuse is ignored or not reported at least 75% of the time. There are many types of abuse, some worse than others, though all cause serious lasting damage to a life.

Abuse can be physical or emotional or both. Eventually the scars and darkness will show Children are not the only victims of abuse. Adults and innocent animals suffer unimaginable abuse as well.

Criminal cases involving abuse go unheard. Many continue to suffer as a result. The lasting trauma from abuse has led to many suicides and suicide attempts.

No one should have to deal with someone else's rage; no one should have to suffer from its impact.

Abuse in this country is on the rise. Not just in America but worldwide. All people have a right to live free of exploitation and abuse.

Everyone in this world is precious. I learned that during my journey to the United States. My trials have not been easy, but I faced them with strength and courage and even faith.

Today, I am an entrepreneur. And guess what? Life, a good life, does not always end with a green card or money or fame.

Life is how you make it! Life is about one thing: INNER PEACE. Only then can one live and lead a sane and productive and creative life.

Education is also very important. Education is a major source of inspiration and motivation.

First thing each morning I ask myself, what kind of day do I wish to have? Visualize what you really want.

Growing up with abuse is toxic; hiding pain does nothing but make the scarring worse.

If you are a victim of abuse, find a way to get your voice heard. Someone (other than you) needs to know before things get worse.

Reaching out sooner rather than later is the key. *Abuse* is defined as anything that is harmful, injurious or offensive to a person, animal and, for that matter, the environment.

You may be a victim of physical abuse or mental abuse. Or both. Traumatizing moments will stick like glue. I was subjected to all kinds of abuse because I loved differently.

Don't let **fear** stop you from speaking out.

I encourage you to share what you are facing with someone you trust.

Now you know what I had to face. Know that these moments don't last forever. Reach out for help now.

Resources: Child Abuse

CHILDREN'S BUREAU

Administration for Children and Families

U.S. Department of Health & Human Services

330 C Street, S.W.

Washington, D.C. 20201

The Children's Bureau (CB) partners with federal, state, tribal and local agencies to improve the overall health and well-being of our nation's children and families and offers the following programs:

- **Promoting Safe and Stable Families**
  - o **The Court Improvement program**
- **Child Abuse Prevention and Treatment Act (CAPTA)**
- **CAPTA discretionary fund**
- **CAPTA state grants**
- **Community-Based Child Abuse Prevention (CBCAP) Grants**

- **The Children's Justice Act (CJA)**

- **National Conferences on Child Abuse & Neglect**

CHILD WELFARE INFORMATION GATEWAY

1-800=394-3366

info@childwelfare.gov

Providing the following list of resources:

ARCH National Respite Network and Resource Center

4016 Oxford Street

Annandale, Virginia 22003

Phone: (703) 256-9578

The mission of the ARCH National Respite Network and Resource Center is to assist and promote the development of quality respite and crisis care programs; to help families locate respite and crisis care services in their communities; and to serve as a strong voice for respite in all forums.

American Academy of Pediatrics

345 Park Boulevard

National Headquarters

Itasca, Illinois 60143

Phone: (202) 247-8600

Phone: (800) 433-9016

Fax: (202) 393-6137, (847) 434-8000

Email: kidsdocs@aap.org

The **Healthy Children** website offers tips and training for parents on a variety of issues such as safety and injury prevention, mental health, and child development. For more information, see http://www. healthychildren.org/.

American Professional Society on the Abuse of Children

1706 E. Broad Street

Columbus, Ohio 43203

Phone: (614) 827-1321

Toll-Free: (877) 402-7722

Fax: (614) 251-6005

Email: apsac@apsac.org

http://www.apsac.org

General Scope: The American Professional Society on the Abuse of Children (APSAC) addresses all facets of the professional response to child maltreatment: prevention, assessment, intervention, and treatment.

American Psychological Association

750 First Street, NE

Washington, District of Columbia 20002

Veemala Victoria Persaud

Phone: (202) 336-5500

Toll-Free: (800) 374-2721

https://www.apa.org

The APA Violence Prevention Office (VPO) coordinates APA's activities related to violence and injury prevention, and treatment on topics associated with child maltreatment, trauma, media violence, and youth violence. VPO major functions are: (a) Coordination of the development, implementation, and evaluation of two major programs: the ACT/Raising Safe Kids Program (parenting skills training and child maltreatment prevention program) and The Effective Providers for Child Victims of Violence Program (training for mental health and other professionals on trauma, assessment tools and treatment models for children victimized by violence); (b) Development of training and educational materials, technical assistance and training to professionals and organizations participating in both programs; (c) Dissemination of research-based knowledge, information, and materials to professionals and the general public on violence, prevention and related topics through Web (www.actagainstviolence.apa.org), Facebook page www. Facebook.com/ACTRaisingSafeKids and other social media outlets; (d) Collaboration with other national associations, national collaboratives, and federal agencies to promote the contributions of psychology and psychologists to the understanding and prevention of violence.

Annie E. Casey Foundation

701 St. Paul Street

Baltimore, Maryland 21202

Phone: (410) 547-6600

Fax: (410) 547-6624

https://www.facebook.com/AnnieECaseyFndn?ref=ts

https://twitter.com/aecfnews

http://www.youtube.com/user/AnnieECaseyFound

The Annie E. Casey Foundation works to build better futures for disadvantaged children and their families. The primary mission of the Foundation is to foster public policies, human service reforms, and community supports that meet the needs of today's vulnerable children and families.

Center for the Study of Social Policy

1575 Eye Street NW

Suite 500

Washington, District of Columbia 20005

Phone: (202) 371-1565

Fax: (202) 371-1472

http://www.cssp.org/

https://www.facebook.com/pages/Center-for-the-Study-of-Social-Policy/119688008090715https://twitter.com/CtrSocialPolicy

The mission of the Center for the Study of Social Policy (CSSP) is to develop and promote public policies and practices that support and strengthen families and help communities produce equal opportunities and better futures for children.

The Center coordinates the national Strengthening Families initiative which is being implemented in over half of all States. Strengthening Families engages early childhood programs and other unusual partners in preventing child abuse and neglect by building five, research-based, Protective Factors that are shown to be correlated with reduced incidence of child abuse and neglect. The Strengthening Families National Network provides tools, peer support, technical assistance, and other resources for States implementing Strengthening Families. For more information about this initiative, please see http:// www.strengtheningfamilies.net

Chapin Hall Center for Children

1313 East 60th Street

Chicago, Illinois 60637

Phone: (773) 256-5100

Fax: (773) 753-5940

http://www.chapinhall.org/

Chapin Hall is a research and development center focusing on policies, practices, and programs affecting children and the families and communities in which they live. The Center devotes special attention to children facing significant problems such as abuse or neglect, poverty, and mental or physical illnesses, and to the service systems designed to address these problems.

Child Welfare Information Gateway

Children's Bureau/ACYF

330 C Street, S.W

Washington, District of Columbia 20201

Toll-Free: (800) 394-3366

Email: info@childwelfare.gov

http://www.childwelfare.gov

https://www.facebook.com/childwelfare

Child Welfare Information Gateway connects professionals and the general public to information and resources targeted to the safety, permanency, and well-being of children and families.

A service of the Children's Bureau, Administration for Children and Families, U.S. Department of Health and Human Services, Child Welfare Information Gateway provides access to programs, research, laws and policies, training resources, statistics, and much more.

Child Welfare League of America

Headquarters

727 15th St. NW

12th Floor

Washington, District of Columbia 20005

Phone: (202) 688-4200

Fax: (202) 833-1689

Email: cwla@cwla.org

http://www.cwla.org/

https://www.facebook.com/CWLAUpdates

The Child Welfare League of America (CWLA) is the oldest national organization serving vulnerable children, youth, and their families. CWLA provides training, consultation, and technical assistance to child welfare professionals and agencies while also educating the public on emerging issues that affect abused, neglected, and at-risk children. Through its publications, conferences, and teleconferences, CWLA shares information on emerging trends, specific topics in child welfare practice (family foster care, kinship care, adoption, positive youth development), and Federal and State policies.

Childhelp®

4350 E. Camelback Rd.

Bldg F250

Phoenix, Arizona 85018

Phone: (480) 922-8212

Toll-Free: (800) 4AC-HILD

TDD: (800) 2AC-HILD

Fax: (480) 922-7061

http://www.childhelp.org/

https://www.facebook.com/childhelp

https://twitter.com/Childhelp

http://www.youtube.com/childhelponline

Childhelp® is dedicated to helping victims of child abuse and neglect. Childhelp's approach focuses on prevention, intervention and treatment. The Childhelp National Child Abuse Hotline, 1-800-4-A-CHILD®, operates 24 hours a day, seven days a week, and receives calls from throughout the United States, Canada, the U.S. Virgin Islands, Puerto Rico and Guam. Childhelp's programs and services also include residential treatment services; children's advocacy centers; therapeutic foster care; group homes; child abuse prevention, education and training; and the National Day of Hope®, part of National Child Abuse Prevention Month every April.

Circle of Parents

P.O. Box 17982

Richmond, Virginia 23226

Phone: (540) 847-8483

Phone: (804) 308-0841

Email: Circleofparentsac@gmail.com

http://www.circleofparents.org

The mission of the Circle of Parents is to prevent child abuse and neglect and to strengthen families through friendly, supportive, mutual self-help parent support groups and children's programs.

Currently the Circle of Parents national network represents a partnership of parent leaders and 26 statewide organizations in 25 States and Puerto Rico. The organization was formed after a successful collaborative project of Prevent Child Abuse America and the National Family Support Roundtable, which was made possible by the Children's Bureau, Administration on Children, Youth and Families, U.S. Department of Health and Human Services.

The Circle of Parents website provides links to information about the program model, its state network member organizations, training and technical assistance to its membership, parenting resources, and more.

Darkness to Light

> 7 Radcliffe Street
>
> Suite 200
>
> Charleston, South Carolina 29403
>
> Phone: (843) 965-5444
>
> Toll-Free: (866) FOR-LIGH T8663675444
>
> Fax: (843) 965-5449
>
> http://www.darkness2light.org/
>
> https://www.facebook.com/DarknessToLight
>
> https://twitter.com/darkness2light

Darkness to Light is a primary prevention program whose mission is to engage adults in the prevention of child sexual abuse; to reduce the incidence of child sexual abuse nationally through education and public awareness aimed at adults; and to provide adults with information to recognize and react responsibly to child sexual abuse.

Doris Duke Charitable Foundation

650 Fifth Avenue, 19th Floor
New York, New York 10019
Phone: (212) 974-7000
Fax: (212) 974-7590

The mission of the Doris Duke Charitable Foundation's Child Abuse Prevention Program is to protect children from abuse and neglect in order to promote their healthy development.

The program awards grants to organizations to improve parent-child interactions and to increase parents' access to information and services that help prevent child maltreatment before it occurs.

FRIENDS National Center for Community-Based Child Abuse Prevention (CBCAP)

800 Eastowne Drive
Suite 105
Chapel Hill, North Carolina 27514
Phone: (919) 493-1584

http://friendsnrc.org/

FRIENDS National Center for Community-Based Child Abuse Prevention (CBCAP) is a program authorized by Title II of the Child Abuse Prevention and Treatment Act that provides Federal funds to a lead agency in each State designated by the Governor to provide leadership for and support to child abuse prevention programs and activities in the State. FRIENDS assists CBCAP State Lead Agencies meet the requirements of their funding through the development of written resources and the provision of training and technical assistance.

Gundersen National Child Protection Training Center

175 West Mark Street

Maxwell Hall, 2nd Floor

Winona, Minnesota 55987

Phone: (614) 834-7946

http://www.gundersenhealth.org/ncptc

The Gundersen National Child Protection Training Center (NCPTC) works to end child abuse, neglect and other forms of child maltreatment in three generations through education, training, awareness, prevention, advocacy and the pursuit of justice. The Center promotes reformation of current training practices by providing an educational curriculum to current and future front-line child protection professionals around the nation so that they will be prepared to recognize and report the abuse of a child. NCPTC also focuses on prevention, advocacy, and education through the Jacob Wetterling

Resource Center, the Center for Effective Discipline, and the National Association to Prevent the Sexual Abuse of Children. test

National Alliance of Children's Trust and Prevention Funds

5712 30th Avenue NE

Seattle, Washington 98105

Phone: (206) 526-1221

Fax: (206) 526-0220

Email: info@ctfalliance.org

The National Alliance of Children's Trust and Prevention Funds (ACT) initiates and engages in national efforts that assist state Children's Trust and Prevention Funds in strengthening families to prevent child abuse and neglect. This includes promoting and supporting a system of services, laws, practices, and attitudes that supports families by enabling them to provide their children with a safe, healthy, and nurturing childhood.

National Association for the Education of Young Children

1509 16th Street NW

Washington, District of Columbia 20036

Phone: (202) 232-8777

Toll-Free: (800) 424-2460

Fax: (202) 328-1846

Email: naeyc@naeyc.org

http://www.naeyc.org/

https://www.facebook.com/NAEYC

https://twitter.com/naeyc

The National Association for the Education of Young Children (NAEYC) is the leading membership association for those working with and on behalf of children from birth through age 8.

NAEYC convenes thought leaders, teachers and other practitioners, researchers, and other stakeholders and sets standards of excellence for programs and teachers in early childhood education. NAEYC members include teachers, paraeducators, center directors, trainers, college educators, families of young children, and the public at large. Membership is open to all individuals who share a desire to serve and act on behalf of the needs and rights of all young children.

National Center for Children in Poverty

215 West 125th Street 3rd Floor

154 Haven Avenue

New York, New York 10027

Phone: (646) 284-9600

Fax: (646) 284-9623

http://www.nccp.org/

The National Center for Children in Poverty (NCCP) is a public policy center dedicated to promoting the economic security, health, and well-being of America's low income families and children. Using research to inform policy and practice, NCCP seeks to advance family-oriented solutions and the strategic use of public resources at the State and national levels to ensure positive outcomes for the next generation.

National Center on Shaken Baby Syndrome

1433 North Highway 1075 West

Suite 110

Farmington, Utah 84025

Phone: (801) 447-9360

Fax: (801) 447-9364

Email: mail@dontshake.org

http://www.dontshake.org/

General Scope: The National Center on Shaken Baby Syndrome (NCSBS) offers information on shaken baby syndrome, shaken baby syndrome prevention programs, and training for professionals and parents nationwide.

National Child Abuse & Neglect Technical Assistance and Strategic Dissemination Center (CANTASD) @Impaq International

4350 East West Highway

Suite 1100

Bethesda, Maryland 20814

Phone: 240-744-7071

Email: hello@cantasd.org

http://www.cantasd.org/index.html

The National Child Abuse and Neglect Technical Assistance and Strategic Dissemination Center (CANTASD) is a service of the Children's Bureau, Office on Child Abuse & Neglect. Its focus is the "front end" of the child welfare system, creating resources and supporting peer learning activities—including the National Conferences on Child Abuse & Neglect—for those engaged in primary and secondary prevention, child protective services and investigation, and multidisciplinary and interagency collaborations to promote the safety and well-being of children, youth, and families.

National Children's Alliance

516 C Street, NE

Washington, District of Columbia 20002

Phone: (202) 548-0090

Toll-Free: (800)239-9950

Fax: (202) 548-0099

http://www.nationalchildrensalliance.org/

https://www.facebook.com/NationalChildrensAlliance

General Scope: The National Children's Alliance is a nonprofit membership organization that provides training, technical assistance, and networking opportunities to communities seeking to plan, establish, and improve Children's Advocacy Centers. These Centers further the goal of serving abused children through a comprehensive approach to services for victims and their families.

National Court Appointed Special Advocate Association

100 West Harrison Street

North Tower, Suite 500

Seattle, Washington 98119

Phone: (206) 774-7250

Toll-Free: (800) 628-3233

http://www.CASAforChildren.org

https://www.facebook.com/CASAforChildren

https://twitter.com/NationalCASA

http://www.youtube.com/casaforchildren

Court Appointed Special Advocates (CASA) for Children is a network of 933 community-based programs that recruit, train and support citizen-volunteers to advocate for the best interests of abused and neglected children in courtrooms and communities. Volunteer advocates—empowered directly by the courts—offer judges the critical information they need to ensure that each child's rights and needs are being attended to while in foster care.

National Fatherhood Initiative

12410 Milestone Center Drive

Suite 600

Germantown, Maryland 20874

Phone: (301) 948-0599

Fax: (301) 948-6776

https://twitter.com/thefatherfactor

The National Fatherhood Initiative works to improve the well-being of children by increasing the proportion of children growing up with involved, responsible, and committed fathers.

National Indian Child Welfare Association

5100 SW Macadam Avenue

Suite 300

Portland, Oregon 97239

Phone: (503) 222-4044

Email: info@nicwa.org

http://www.nicwa.org

https://www.facebook.com/NativeChildren?v=feed&story_
fbid=111114601179

https://twitter.com/NativeChildren

The National Indian Child Welfare Association (NICWA) functions as the only Native American organization focused specifically on issues of child abuse and neglect and tribal capacity to prevent and respond effectively to these problems. NICWAprovide workshops and training programs, using culturally appropriate NICWA developed resources, including training materials, curricula, and books. NICWA also offers technical assistance and training on child care, family preservation, and substance abuse.

National Network of Family Support and Strengthening Networks

95 Washburn Street

San Francisco, California 94103

Phone: (415) 730-5310

Email: info@nationalfamilysupportnetwork.org

https://nationalfamilysupportnetwork.org/

Founded in 2011, the National Network of Family Support & Strengthening Networks (NNFSSN) is a membership-based organization comprised of statewide networks that focus on strengthening and supporting families. Each of these networks consists of two or more Family Resource Centers or Family Strengthening organizations. The mission of the NNFSSN is to connect statewide networks across the United States to promote quality practice, peer learning, mutual support, and effective policies and systems that support positive outcomes for children, families, and communities.

National Resource Center for Healthy Marriage and Families

9300 Lee Highway

Fairfax, Virginia 22031

Toll-Free: 1-866-916-4672

Email: info@HealthyMarriageandFamilies.org

The National Resource Center for Healthy Marriage and Families promotes the value of healthy marriage and relationship education (MRE) skills and encourages their integration into safety-net service systems as a holistic approach to strengthening families.

Nurse-Family Partnership

1900 Grant Street

Suite 400

Denver, Colorado 80203

Phone: (303) 327-4240

Toll-Free: (866) 864-5226

Fax: (303) 327-4260

Email: info@nursefamilypartnership.org

http://www.nursefamilypartnership.org/

The Nurse-Family Partnership represents an approach to the long-established service strategy of the home visiting model that improves the health and social functioning of low income, first-time mothers, their babies, and families.

Parents Anonymous® Inc.

675 West Foothill Boulevard

Suite 220

Claremont, California 91711-3475

Phone: (909) 621-6184

Fax: (909) 625-6304

Email: Parentsanonymous@parentsanonymous.org

http://www.parentsanonymous.org

https://www.facebook.com/NationalParentHelpline

https://twitter.com/parenthelpline

http://www.youtube.com/parenthelpline

Parents Anonymous® Inc. is a family strengthening organization dedicated to the prevention of child abuse and neglect. Parents Anonymous® Inc. operates numerous programs and initiatives, including an international **Network** of accredited organizations that implement Parents Anonymous® groups and complementary children and youth programs based on a mutual support-shared leadership® model. In addition, Parents Anonymous ® provides many services, including specialized trainings, customized technical assistance, public awareness and outreach strategies, and evaluation services to States, counties, and community-based organizations on a wide range of topics related to children and families.

Prevent Child Abuse America

228 S. Wabash

10th Floor

Chicago, Illinois 60604

Phone: (312) 663-3520

Fax: (312) 939-8962

Email: mailbox@preventchildabuse.org

http://www.preventchildabuse.org/

https://www.facebook.com/pages/Prevent-Child-Abuse-America/14893558501

http://www.youtube.com/pcaamerica

Prevent Child Abuse America (PCAA) is committed to promoting legislation, policies, and programs that help prevent child abuse and neglect, support healthy childhood development, and strengthen families. Working with State chapters, PCCA provides leadership to promote and implement prevention efforts at the national and local levels.

PCAA's research arm is the National Center on Child Abuse Prevention Research and Resources http://preventchildabuse.org/resources/. The Center provides a link between research and practice by developing and evaluating prevention strategies, and by disseminating information about child abuse maltreatment and its prevention across the country.

Search Institute

The Banks Building

615 First Avenue NW -- Suite 125

Minneapolis, Minnesota 55413

Phone: (612) 376-8955

Toll-Free: (800) 888-7828

Email: si@search-institute.org

http://www.search-institute.org

https://www.facebook.com/SearchInstitute

https://twitter.com/searchinstitute

http://www.youtube.com/searchinstitute

Search Institute conducts research to identify what children and adolescents need to become caring, healthy, and responsible adults. The Institute also provides resources to apply this knowledge and to motivate and equip others in ensuring young people are valued and that they thrive.

Stop It Now!

351 Pleasant Street

Suite B319

Northampton, Massachusetts 01060

Phone: (413) 587-3500

Toll-Free: (888) 773-8368

Email: info@stopitnow.org

http://www.StopItNow.org

https://www.facebook.com/StopItNow

https://twitter.com/stopitnow

http://www.youtube.com/wecanstopitnow

Stop It Now!® prevents the sexual abuse of children by mobilizing adults, families and communities to take action before a child is harmed. Stop It Now! provides support, information and resources for adults to take responsibility for creating safer communities.

The Full Frame Initiative

308 Main Street

Suite 2A

Greenfield, Massachusetts 01301

Phone: (413) 773-3400

Email: info@fullframeinitiative.org

http://fullframeinitiative.org/

The Full Frame Initiative (FFI) is a national nonprofit organization that works to break cycles of poverty and violence through systems change. FFI has discovered the common DNA among the organizations that effectively serve people with multiple challenges — lasting change occurs when people are supported in the full frame of their lives. Many more organizations would choose to operate with a Full Frame Approach, but they are stymied by rules, regulations and other barriers present throughout the social service system. In partnership with practical visionaries in government, nonprofits, philanthropy and communities,

FFI removes systemic barriers to full frame practice, allowing more people and communities to thrive.

ZERO TO THREE

National Center for Infants, Toddlers and Families

2000 M Street NW, Suite 200

Suite 200

Washington, District of Columbia 20036

Phone: (202) 638-1144

Toll-Free: (800) 899-4301

http://www.zerotothree.org

https://www.facebook.com/ZEROTOTHREE

Zero to Three's mission is to promote the healthy development of our nation's infants and toddlers by supporting and strengthening families, communities, and those who work on their behalf. Zero to Three is dedicated to advancing current knowledge, promoting beneficial policies and practices, communicating research and best practices to a wide variety of audiences, and providing training, technical assistance, and leadership development.

Resources: Transgender Issues and Advocacy

American Civil Liberties Union (ACLU)

listing 185 blogs and posts about transgender rights

125 Broad Street, 18th Floor

New York NY 10004

212-549-2500

National Center for Transgender Equality

(202) 642-4542

ncte@transequality.org1133 19th St NW

Suite 302

Washington D.C. 20036

Samuel Lurie, Transgender Training and Advocacy

Tel: 802-453-5370 x2

Fax: 802-453-7096

Email: **info@tgtrain.org**

Transgender Advocacy Network (TAN)

www.transadvocacynetwork.org

Transgender Organizations (listed on Glaad, https://www.glaad.org/transgender/resources):

Transgender People in Crisis Can Access these Resources:

The Trevor Project's 24/7/365 Lifeline at 866-4-U-TREVOR (866-488-7386) or TrevorChat, their online instant messaging option, or TrevorText, a text-based support option

The National Suicide Prevention Lifeline at 800-273-TALK (8255)

Trans Lifeline at 877-565-8860

National Center for Transgender Equality (NCTE) (advocacy)

Transgender Law Center (TLC) (legal services and advocacy)

Gender Proud (advocacy)

Sylvia Rivera Law Project (SRLP) (legal services)

Transgender Legal Defense and Education Fund (TLDEF) (legal services)

Massachusetts Transgender Political Coalition (MTPC) (advocacy)

Trans People of Color Coalition (TPOCC) (advocacy)

Trans Women of Color Collective (TWOCC) (advocacy)

Black Trans Advocacy (advocacy)

Trans Latina Coalition (advocacy)

Gender Spectrum (support for families, trans youth, and educators)

Trans Youth Equality Federation (support for families and trans youth)

Trans Youth Family Allies (TYFA) (support for families and trans youth)

TransTech Social Enterprises (economic empowerment)

SPART*A (advocacy for trans military service members)

Transgender American Veterans Association (advocacy for trans veterans)

Suggested Readings

http://www.transfaithonline.org/

Transfaith is a <u>national non-profit</u> that is <u>led by transgender people</u>. We are a multi-tradition, multi-racial, multi-gender organization working to support transgender spiritual/cultural workers and their leadership in community. We work closely with many allied organizations, secular, spiritual, and religious, transgender-led and otherwise.

Readings, sermons and inspirational texts by religious leaders from many faiths.

PFLAG: Transgender Reading List for Adults

<u>Becoming A Visible Man</u> by Jamison Green, Ph.D

<u>Gender Born, Gender Made: Raising Healthy Gender-Nonconforming Children</u> by Diane Ehrensaft, Ph.D.

<u>Gender Outlaw: On Men, Women and the Rest of Us</u> by Kate Bornstein

<u>Helping Your Transgender Teen: A guide for parents</u> by Irwin Krieger

He's My Daughter: A Mother's Journey to Acceptance by Eve Langley

The Last Time I Wore A Dress by Daphne Scholinski

My Husband Betty by Helen Boyd

Raising My Rainbow: Adventures in Raising a Fabulous, Gender Creative Son by Lori Duron

Redefining Realness: My Path to Womanhood, Identity, Love & So Much More by Janet Mock

The Right To Be Out: Sexual Orientation and Gender Identity in America's Public Schools by Stuart Biegel

She's Not the Man I Married: My Life with a Transgender Husband by Helen Boyd

She's Not There: A Life in Two Genders by Jennifer Finney Boylan

The Social Justice Advocate's Handbook: A Guide to Gender by Sam Killerman

Stone Butch Blues by Leslie Feinberg

Stuck in the Middle with You: A Memoir of Parenting in Three Genders by Jennifer Finney

Trans Bodies, Trans Selves: A Resource for the Transgender Community edited by Laura Erickson-Schroth

The Transgender Child: A Handbook for Families and Professionals by Stephanie A. Brill and Rachel Pepper

Transgender Family Law: A Guide to Effective Advocacy by Jennifer Levi & Elizabeth E. Monnin-Browder:

Trans-Kin: A Guide for Family and Friends of Transgender People

(Volume 1) by Dr. Eleanor A. Hubbard (Editor), Cameron T. Whitley (Editor).

Transgender Employment Experiences: Gendered Perceptions and the Law by Kyla Bender- Baird:

Transgender History by Susan Stryker

Transgender Warriors: The Making of History from Joan of Arc to Dennis Rodman by Leslie Feinberg

Transgender Workplace Diversity: Policy Tools, Training Issues and Communication Strategies for HR and Legal Professionalsby Jillian T. Weiss, J.D., Ph.D

Transitions of the Heart edited by Rachel Pepper

Two Spirits, One Heart: A Mother, Her Transgender Son, and Their Journey to Love and Acceptance by Marsha Aizumi with Aiden Aizumi

Whipping Girl: A Transsexual Woman on Sexism and the Scapegoating of Femininity by Julia Serano

The *World Professional Association for Transgender Health* (WPATH), formerly known as the (Harry Benjamin International Gender Dysphoria Association (HBIGDA), is a 501(c)(3) non-profit, interdisciplinary professional and educational organization devoted to transgender health provides the following list of recommended reading:

General Transgender Theory & Experience

Mock, Janet (2014). *Redefining Realness: My Path to Womanhood, Identity, Love & So Much More.* New York: Atria.

Girschick, Lori B. (2008). *Transgender Voices: Beyond Women and Men*. Hanover: University Press of New England.

Serano, Julia (2007). *Whipping Girl: A Transsexual Woman on Sexism and the Scapegoating of Femininity*. Emeryville: Seal Press.

Valentine, David (2007). *Imagining Transgender: An Ethnography of a Category*. Durham: Duke University Press.

Stryker, Susan & Aren Aizura, eds. (2013). *The Transgender Studies Reader 2*. New York: Routledge.

Stryker, Susan & Stephen Whittle (2006). *The Transgender Studies Reader*. New York: Routledge.

Suggested Readings (continued)

Valerio, Max Wolf (2006). *The Testosterone Files: My Hormonal and Social Transformation from Female to Male*. Emeryville: Seal Press.

Green, Jamison (2004). *Becoming a Visible Man*. Nashville: Vanderbilt University Press.

Wilchins, Riki (2004). *Queer Theory, Gender Theory: An Instant Primer*. Los Angeles: Alyson Books.

Rose, Donna (2003). *Wrapped in Blue: A Journey of Discovery – a memoir*. Round Rock: Living Legacy Press.

Namaste, Vivian K. (2000). *Invisible Lives: The Erasure of Transsexual and Transgendered People*. Chicago: University of Chicago Press.

Cromwell, Jason (1999). *Transmen & FTMs: Identities, Bodies, Genders & Sexualities*. Urbana: University of Illinois Press.

Prosser, Jay (1998). *Second Skins: the body narratives of transsexuality.* New York: Columbia University Press.

Bornstein, Kate (1994). *Gender Outlaw: On men, women and the rest of us.* New York: Routledge.

Transgender History

Stryker, Susan (2017). *Transgender History, second edition: The Roots of Today's Revolution.* Berkeley: Seal Press.

Stryker, Susan (2008). *Transgender History.* Berkeley: Seal Press.

Meyerowitz, Joanne (2002). *How Sex Changed: A History of Transsexuality in the United States.* Cambridge: Harvard University Press.

Feinberg, Leslie (1996). *Transgender Warriors: Making History from Joan of Arc to RuPaul.* Boston: Beacon Press.

Transgender Law & Policy Texts

Levi, Jennifer L., & Monnin-Browder, Elizabeth E. (Eds.) (2012). *Transgender Family Law: A Guide to Effective Advocacy.* Bloomington: Authorhouse

.Bender-Baird, Kyla (2011). *Transgender Employment Experiences: Gendered Perceptions and the Law.* Albany: State University of New York Press.

Weiss, Jillian T. (2007). *Transgender Workplace Diversity: Policy*

Tools, Training Issues, and Communication Strategies for HR and Legal Professionals. North Charleston: Booksurge Publishing.

Currah, Paisley, Juang, Richard. M., and Minter, Shannon P. (Eds.) (2006). *Transgender Rights*. Minneapolis: University of Minnesota Press.

Health, Medical, and Psychology Texts

Witten, Tarynn M., and Eyler, A. Evan (2012). *Gay, Lesbian, Bisexual & Transgender Aging: Challenges in Research, Practice & Policy*. Baltimore: The Johns Hopkins University Press.

Ehrensaft, Diane (2011). *Gender Born, Gender Made: Raising Healthy Gender-Nonconforming Children*. New York: The Experiment Publishing.

Ettner, Randi, Monstrey, Stan, & Eyler, A. Evan (Eds.) (2007). *Principles of Transgender Medicine and Surgery*. New York: The Haworth Press. Second Edition (2016), Ettner, Monstrey, & Coleman, Eli (Eds.)

Lev, Arlene Istar (2004). *Transgender Emergence: Therapeutic Guidelines for Working With Gender-Variant People and their Families*. Binghamton, NY: Haworth Clinical Practice Press.

Children and Adolescent (for Adults, by non-clinical authors)

Brill, Stephanie and Pepper, Rachel (2008). *The Transgender Child: A Handbook for Families and Professionals*. San Francisco: Cleis Press.

Beam, Chris (2007). *Transparent: Love, Family, and Living the T with Transgender Teenagers.* Orlando: Harcourt, Inc.

Intersex-related

Greenberg, Julie (2012). *Intersexuality and the Law: Why Sex Matters.* New York: NYU Press.

Karkazis, Katrina (2008). *Fixing Sex: Intersex, Medical Authority, and Lived Experience.* Durham, Duke University Press.

Preves, Sharon E. (2003). *Intersex and Identity: The Contested Self.* New Brunswick: Rutgers University Press.

Dreger, Alice Domurat (1998). *Hermaphrodites and the Medical Invention of Sex.* Cambridge: Harvard University Press.

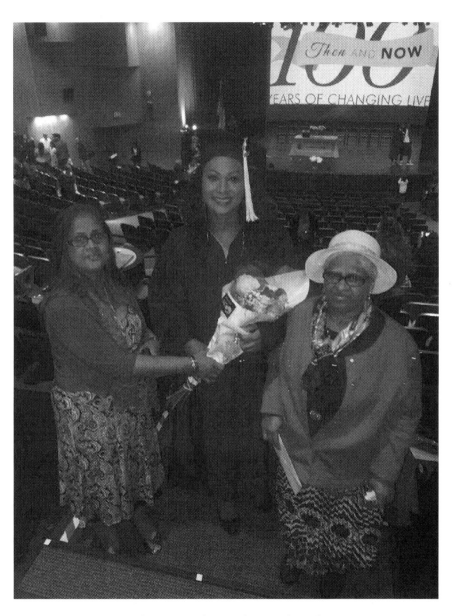

With my Mother and Grandmother

My Mother

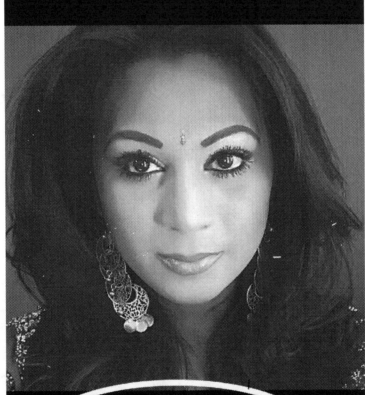

Printed in the United States
By Bookmasters